MARK

"Drawing on ancient and contemporary scholarship, Christopher Skinner offers newcomers a concise yet comprehensive entrée into this Gospel's major themes and their religious origins. Due to its clarity and balanced judgment, I know of no better one-volume introduction."

—*Clifton Black*, Otto A. Piper Professor Emeritus of Biblical Theology, Princeton Theological Seminary

"In this highly engaging guide, Skinner saves us from miles of missteps by showing us how to listen closely and let Mark speak for himself. He not only explores distinct topics that frame Mark's narrative but also shows how they overlap in subtle and surprising ways, empowering us to interpret this Gospel for ourselves. Laypersons, students, and scholars will all benefit from this refreshing analysis of the key themes that propelled the first written Gospel."

—*James Barker*, Associate Professor of New Testament, Western Kentucky University

"With remarkable clarity, Dr. Christopher Skinner introduces a wide array of issues and interpretive approaches important for understanding the Gospel of Mark. Throughout careful explorations of Mark's presentations of Jesus's identity, the kingdom of God, and discipleship, Skinner models the adage to which he encourages readers: 'Let Mark be Mark.' This theologically nuanced, conscientiously contextualized, and attentive reading of Mark's narrative will be a resource which students of Scripture, from undergraduates to seasoned interpreters, will find worth returning to again and again."

—*Kara Lyons-Pardue*, Professor of New Testament, Point Loma Nazarene University

"Mark's Gospel has lived many lives, but it might just be living its best life now—at the heart of contemporary debates about Christian origins and as a testing ground for new methods in biblical studies. However, this surge of attention brings along a daunting swell of secondary literature; where does one turn to get their bearings? Thankfully, we now have a clear answer. Skinner's reliable and engaging volume is an ideal companion for students and scholars alike; this book will be my go-to introduction to Mark for years to come."

—*Max Botner,* Associate Professor of
Biblical Studies, Jessup University

"Skinner succeeds in his aim to 'let Mark be Mark.' With clarity, historical grounding, and scholarly rigor, he traces Mark's presentation of Jesus as Messiah and Son of God, the dynamics of the kingdom of God, and the complex nature of discipleship—making this an invaluable resource for preaching, teaching, and serious study."

—*Elizabeth Shively,* Professor of Christian
Scriptures, George W. Truett Theological
Seminary, Baylor University

"Informed, up-to-date, lively, and accessible—this is an excellent guide to Markan themes for students and pastors alike. A very handy little volume."

—*Helen K. Bond,* Professor of Christian
Origins, University of Edinburgh

2

WORD
BIBLICAL
THEMES

NEW

MARK

CHRISTOPHER W. SKINNER

NIJAY K. GUPTA, SERIES EDITOR

ZONDERVAN
ACADEMIC

ZONDERVAN ACADEMIC

Mark, Volume 2

Copyright © 2025 by Christopher W. Skinner

Published in Grand Rapids, Michigan, by Zondervan. Zondervan is a registered trademark of The Zondervan Corporation, L.L.C., a wholly owned subsidiary of HarperCollins Christian Publishing, Inc.

Requests for information should be addressed to customercare@harpercollins.com.

Zondervan titles may be purchased in bulk for educational, business, fundraising, or sales promotional use. For information, please email SpecialMarkets@Zondervan.com.

Library of Congress Cataloging-in-Publication Data

Names: Skinner, Christopher W., author.
Title: Mark / Christopher W. Skinner.
Description: Grand Rapids, Michigan: Zondervan Academic, [2025] | Series: New word biblical themes; 2 | Includes index.
Identifiers: LCCN 2024059320 (print) | LCCN 2024059321 (ebook) | ISBN 9780310126850 (paperback) | ISBN 9780310126867 (ebook)
Subjects: LCSH: Bible. Mark—Commentaries.
Classification: LCC BS2585.53 .S57 2025 (print) | LCC BS2585.53 (ebook) | DDC 226.3/07—dc23/eng/20250228
LC record available at https://lccn.loc.gov/2024059320
LC ebook record available at https://lccn.loc.gov/2024059321

Cover design: Tammy Johnson
Interior design: Sara Colley

Printed in the United States of America

25 26 27 28 29 TRM 10 9 8 7 6 5 4 3 2 1

For

Sandra Long Womack (1952–2022)
Joseph Ray Long Jr. (1960–2022)

With sorrow over your absence in this world but
gratitude for your enduring presence in our lives.

Contents

Series Preface

In 1982, F. F. Bruce's 1–2 Thessalonians commentary was among the first volumes to appear in the now highly esteemed Word Biblical Commentary series (1982–). A handful of years later, the Word Biblical Themes series began publication with Leslie Allen's Psalms and Ralph Martin's Philippians volumes, both printed in 1987. The WBT series was designed to supplement the WBC by offering short discussions of the most important themes in each biblical book. While the WBC volumes were technical and lengthy, focusing on an audience of scholars, the WBT series was meant to distill the key messages of biblical texts to help students and pastors as they present Scripture's testimony to form churches today.

Over the last forty-five years the Word Biblical Commentary series has almost reached completion of its fifty-two volumes, and some older volumes have been revised. However, the original Word Biblical Themes series only managed to produce fifteen volumes between 1987 and 1991. Therefore, we are pleased to now carry on the original vision of this supplement series with *New* Word Biblical Themes, allowing a new generation of scholars to explore the most crucial theological themes in each book of Scripture. These concise guides will inform and enhance Bible study, Christian teaching, and faithful preaching of the Word of God.

The New Word Biblical Themes offers the following features:

- Reliable research from a diverse group of expert scholars
- An up-to-date academic summary of basic issues of background, structure, and content for each biblical book
- Focused study of each biblical book, discussing the most important theological themes
- Insight into the "big picture" of a book of the Bible by understanding what topics and concerns were most important to the biblical writers
- Thoughtful reflection on theological and moral issues facing the church today by showing readers how the biblical writers approached similar issues in their day
- Reading recommendations for those who want to explore topics in more depth

We hope that readers will be blessed by the expertise of the series contributors, enlightened by concise and clear thematic discussions, challenged by fresh ideas and approaches, and encouraged in their own reading of the Bible as a text full of wisdom.

Nijay K. Gupta

Author Preface

Over the past nineteen years I have had the privilege of serving in various institutions of higher learning. During that period, writing has been an ever-present companion. However, without warning, my ability to put pen to paper arrived at a screeching halt sometime in early 2019 and persisted for almost three years. It feels strange to say now, but I have told colleagues and friends that it was almost as if I had *forgotten how to write*. I still cannot fully account for what caused this frustrating season, though there is little doubt that other external factors also contributed to this malaise. In March of 2020 the entire world went into a two-year shutdown sparked by a once-in-a-generation, worldwide pandemic. That event alone caused enough collective anxiety to last us another decade. Later that September, my younger son, Drew, was unexpectedly diagnosed with type one diabetes, which produced a series of cascading emotions that we are still navigating today. Amidst all of this struggle, I wondered whether this book (or any other) might ever see the light of day. It is on that note that I choose to celebrate the publication of this work.

I was fortunate to be raised in a small town in southeastern Virginia around a supportive extended family that contributed significantly to the person I am today. From my family I learned a great deal about the world and about my place in that world. In early 2022, while I was in the middle of writing this book, two important figures from that extended family departed this earth—both unexpectedly and both much too soon.

My mother's younger sister, Sandra (my Aunt Sandy) was a lovely soul who read me stories and sang me to sleep when I was a child. I have many fond memories of laughing and singing with her while sitting with her family in the cool breeze of their backyard on the Currituck Sound in North Carolina during my teenage years. Throughout high school and college I worked alongside her husband—my Uncle Keith—in their family landscaping business, a setting in which I learned much about the value of hard work. I am grateful for all of these memories with her and for the impact she had upon my life. Aunt Sandy lived long enough to meet and fall in love with her first grandchild, Tristan Keith, who was born on her last birthday on this earth. Now, in the words of my mother, "we have Tristan here to ease our pain, if only a little." We see in him her hopes and dreams for the future, and that is something we can hold onto.

Six weeks prior to the passing of my Aunt Sandy, my mother's only brother, my Uncle Joey, also died unexpectedly. He was only sixty-one. When I was in kindergarten, we were asked to describe our favorite person in the world. On that wide-ruled, green paper they give to five-year-old children, I wrote about my Uncle Joey. He was easily my favorite person. As I grew older, I admired him for his athletic abilities, his coaching prowess, his life-of-the-party personality, and his ability to somehow infuse every moment with excitement and humor. I wanted to emulate every single one of those traits. He introduced me to musical influences that I would not have known otherwise, and I have carried the love of those with me throughout my adult life. He was there when I graduated high school, moved into my first dorm room, graduated from college, got married, and moved away to start my own family. He was always there. In 2009 I lost my job and was forced to move from my home in Baltimore to live with my in-laws in Virginia Beach. Tara and I were broke and Christmas was fast approaching. He called and asked if he could meet me at Starbucks, and when I got there, he handed me an envelope filled with an enormous wad of cash that enabled me to buy Christmas presents for our three children that year. We would not have been able to afford it otherwise. I am still moved when I think of that generosity. I could go on telling stories, but it would not be enough. It is not possible for me to quantify my uncle's impact upon my life. He was, quite simply, my lifelong hero, and the grief from his loss remains with me. Since he left us, barely a day has passed where I have not thought of him or wished for one more opportunity to speak with him. I am deeply grateful for all of my memories with my Uncle Joey and for his impact on so many areas of my life.

Against the backdrop of so much personal angst and grief over these past few years, I happily observe the arrival of this book by dedicating it to the memory of my Aunt Sandy and my Uncle Joey with gratitude for their love and influence. Their physical absence has not diminished their enduring presence in my life.

Christopher W. Skinner
Evanston, Illinois
September 2023

Abbreviations

1 En.	1 Enoch
1QS	Rule of the Community
1QSa	The Rule of the Congregation
AB	Anchor Bible
ABRL	Anchor Bible Reference Library
AYBRL	Anchor Yale Bible Reference Library
BBR	*Bulletin for Biblical Research*
BETL	Bibliotheca Ephemeridum Theologicarum Lovaniensium
Bib	*Biblica*
BibInt	Biblical Interpretation Series
BTB	*Biblical Theology Bulletin*
BZNW	Beihefte zur Zeitschrift für die neutestamentliche Wissenschaft
CD	Damascus Document
CurBR	*Currents in Biblical Research*
CBQ	*Catholic Biblical Quarterly*
EC	*Early Christianity*
ECHC	Early Christianity in Its Hellenistic Context
EJL	Early Judaism and Its Literature
ESV	English Standard Version
FRLANT	Forschungen zur Religion und Literatur des Alten und Neuen Testaments

GBS	Guides to Biblical Scholarship
HTR	*Harvard Theological Review*
JAAR	*Journal of the American Academy of Religion*
JAOS	*Journal of the American Oriental Society*
JBL	*Journal of Biblical Literature*
JGRChJ	*Journal of Greco-Roman Christianity and Judaism*
JR	*Journal of Religion*
JSJSup	Journal for the Study of Judaism Supplement Series
JSNT	*Journal for the Study of the New Testament*
JSNTSup	Journal for the Study of the New Testament Supplement Series
JSJ	*Journal for the Study of Judaism in the Persian, Hellenistic and Roman Periods*
JTS	*Journal of Theological Studies*
LCL	Loeb Classical Library
LNTS	Library of New Testament Studies
LSTS	Library of Second Temple Studies
LQ	*Lutheran Quarterly*
LXX	Septuagint
MAAR	*Memoirs of the American Academy in Rome*
Neot	*Neotestamentica*
NETS	New English Translation of the Septuagint
NovT	*Novum Testamentum*
NRSV	New Revised Standard Version
NRSVue	New Revised Standard Version, Updated Edition
NTL	New Testament Library
NTS	*New Testament Studies*
Pss. Sol.	Psalms of Solomon
RBS	Resources for Biblical Study
RevQ	*Revue de Qumran*
SBLDS	Society of Biblical Literature Dissertation Series
SBLMS	Society of Biblical Literature Monograph Series

SJT   *Scottish Journal of Theology*
SNTSMS   Society for New Testament Studies Monograph
             Series
WUNT   Wissenschaftliche Untersuchungen zum Neuen
             Testament

About This Book

This volume is a part of the New Word Biblical Themes series published by Zondervan Academic. A brief explanation of and rationale for the book's contents will help orient the reader to what follows. The format of the books in this series follows a prescribed pattern. The first chapter of the volumes published in this series is devoted to a coverage of introductory matters on our assigned text, in this case, the Gospel of Mark. The second chapter is supposed to focus on tracing the role our text has played in discussions within Christian theology. (It will become clear fairly quickly that Mark's role in the development of Christian theology is a little more difficult to trace than other New Testament writings treated by this series.) After these two chapters, the remainder of the book is devoted to a treatment of themes unique to the Gospel of Mark—thus New Word Biblical *Themes*. In what follows, I have attempted to provide a faithful overview of the most important introductory and historical concerns while tracing some of the important literary and theological themes across the Second Gospel. There are, of course, too many themes in Mark to cover them all fully in such a brief book. Therefore, in some cases, I have included in the discussion of a major theme (e.g., the kingdom of God, which spans two chapters) multiple related concerns (e.g.,

Markan literary style, theological incomprehension, theory of parables, etc.). It is my hope that this text will prove useful for those beginning their study of the Gospel of Mark and for those returning to their study who need an informed opinion about the text.

CHAPTER 1

Beginning Our Journey with the Gospel of Mark

MARK: OUR FIRST WRITTEN GOSPEL

Few achievements in the history of earliest Christianity can rival the significance of introducing the first written gospel to the world. That is exactly what the author of Mark's Gospel accomplished. Our best evidence suggests that the Gospel of Mark was the first written text to narrate the life and ministry of Jesus. Making use of biographical and literary features already known within certain segments of the Greco-Roman world, Mark crafted a story that became early Christianity's foundational narrative of the life of Jesus.[1] The Gospel relays the story of the Messiah and Son of God (1:1; 8:29–30; 9:7; 15:39), who calls disciples (1:16–20; 2:13–17; 3:13–19), speaks in mysteries (4:10–20), preaches in parables (3:23–27; 4:1–9, 21–34; 12:1–9; 13:28–31), casts out unclean spirits (1:21–28;

---

1. There is debate as to what ancient genre the gospels represent. Many agree that the gospels most closely approximate the genre known as Greco-Roman biography (or *bios*). For the fullest exposition of this thesis, see Richard Burridge, *What Are the Gospels? A Comparison with Graeco-Roman Biography*, 25th anniv. ed. (Waco, TX: Baylor University Press, 2020); see also Helen Bond, *The First Biography of Jesus: Genre and Meaning in Mark's Gospel* (Grand Rapids: Eerdmans, 2020). Others argue that the gospels represent a sort of genre mosaic that incorporates features of multiple ancient genres operating in the Greco-Roman world at the time. For more on this, see the excursus below.

3:11–12; 5:1–20), heals the sick and suffering (1:29–32, 40–45; 2:1–12; 3:1–6; 5:21–43; 6:53–56; 7:24–30, 31–37; 8:22–26; 9:14–29; 10:46–52), and ultimately gives his life as a ransom for many (10:45; 15:1–47). If this sounds like the Jesus you have come to know, then you largely have the Gospel of Mark to thank. In the span of several decades after Mark's Gospel appeared, early Christian writers generated over half a dozen gospels, three of which also found their way into the Christian canon.[2] You might say that Mark "broke the story" of Jesus to the world. Despite this primacy of position, the Gospel of Mark was long overlooked by readers and commentators in favor of the other canonical Gospels, especially Matthew and John.[3] Only within the last two centuries has the Gospel of Mark received even a small portion of the attention it deserves. In this book I hope to continue that trend by highlighting Mark's important contributions to our knowledge about Jesus and to developments within Christian teaching and theology.

The present chapter situates Mark's Gospel in its historical context. We need to consider several critical issues here, including questions of dating (When did the Gospel appear?), authorship (Who wrote the Gospel?), provenance and audience (Where was the Gospel written and for whom?) and finally, purpose (What is Mark trying to accomplish with this story of Jesus?). Once we have covered these concerns, we

---

2. These are the Gospel of Matthew (ca. 75–80 CE), the Gospel of Luke (ca. 80–85 CE), the Gospel of John (ca. 95–100 CE), the Gospel of Thomas (ca. 95–150 CE), Marcion's Gospel (ca. 130–140 CE), the Egerton Gospel (ca. 150 CE), and the Gospel of Peter (ca. 150–160 CE). Beginning in the last quarter of the second century CE and moving forward there is an explosion of gospel texts. While these texts do not all share the same theological outlook, there is no doubt that they owe elements of their structure, content, form, and foci to the Gospel of Mark. For a recent attempt at assigning earlier dates to most of the NT writings, see Jonathan Bernier, *Rethinking the Dates of the New Testament: The Evidence for Early Composition* (Grand Rapids: Baker Academic, 2022).

3. We will discuss this in greater detail in the next chapter.

will be in a much better position to deliberate on the literary and theological issues presented to us by the text itself.

FIGURE 1.1

Excursus

Genre and the Gospels: Are the Gospels *Bioi*?

Today, a majority of NT scholars hold that the canonical Gospels most closely resemble the genre known as Greco-Roman biography or *bios* (plural: *bioi*). These ancient texts usually focused on tracing the major life events of a famous or noteworthy individual (e.g., Julius Caesar, Alexander the Great) with the goal of showing how that person lived a virtuous life and was worthy of being imitated. In his important book, *What Are the Gospels? A Comparison with Graeco-Roman Biography*, Richard Burridge approaches the Gospels from a background in classical studies and argues that, while differing in some important ways, the Gospels appear to be participating in the wider genre of Greco-Roman biography. That thesis has persuaded a great many contemporary scholars of the NT.

However, not everyone is convinced that the Gospels are examples of Greco-Roman biography. Even advocates of that position acknowledge that the Gospels depart from some of the generic elements associated with *bioi*. Other scholars recognize that, while incorporating some elements of the *bios* genre, the Gospels also appear to draw upon literary and rhetorical tropes that appear in other genres within the ancient Greco-Roman world. For a helpful example of this approach, see Harold W. Attridge, "Genre Bending in the Fourth Gospel," *JBL* 121.1 (2002): 3–21. It is safe to say that this question is still up for debate in the current landscape of scholarship.

HISTORICAL QUESTIONS

When Did Mark's Gospel Appear?

Before we consider the specifics related to dating Mark's appearance, it might be prudent to step back and think briefly about the chronology of the New Testament (hereafter, NT) writings in general. For the casual reader of the NT, it might seem obvious that the book should begin with stories about Jesus. He is, after all, the foundational figure in the entire collection of writings and the central focus of Christian teaching and proclamation. It is likely, however, that all the undisputed letters of Paul were written before the first Gospel appeared.[4] An awareness of these dates can help us think about the chronological development of the NT writings as a way of appreciating both the date and the significance of Mark's publication.

While we cannot be certain, scholars date Jesus's death to a period between 28–32 CE. Our earliest NT writings— 1 Thessalonians, Galatians, and possibly the Letter of James— all appeared sometime between 45–51 CE. This means there is a span of roughly two decades between the death of Jesus and

---

4. Scholars largely agree that seven letters—1 Thessalonians, Galatians, 1–2 Corinthians, Philemon, Romans, and Philippians—come to us directly from Paul himself. Significant debate surrounds the date and authorship of the remaining six letters. Paul's death is often dated to between 62 and 68 CE, and the four canonical gospels did not emerge until the last three decades of the first century (ca. 70–100 CE).

the appearance of our first extant Christian texts. Scholars believe that much of the material that found its way into early Christian instruction and eventually gospel writing (e.g., hymns, confessions, miracle stories, parables, etc.) circulated orally for multiple decades. It seems probable that some early Christians memorized this material in its different forms. Either by oral performance or liturgical repetition, some of these early Christians transmitted it orally as part of the warp and woof of Christian existence in the first century.

Most scholars believe that the Gospel of Mark appeared shortly before or after 70 CE, nearly four decades after Jesus's death (more on this below). Before this moment, there were *no written texts* narrating the life and ministry of Jesus. At the very least, no such written texts survived. Mark was the first. Thus, it is not hyperbole to affirm that Mark's narrative portrait of Jesus as Christ represents one of *the* foundational achievements within the first Christian century and one that inspired a key stage in the development of early Christianity—the era of the written gospel. Simply stated, the publication of Mark's Gospel provided early Jesus followers with the narrative framework for thinking about Jesus's life and set the stage for others who would tell their own story by incorporating, altering, correcting, or filling in gaps from Mark's story of Jesus. And, while Mark's Gospel laid the groundwork for later gospel writers, it is also important to acknowledge that this text emerged only after several decades had passed in the nascent Christian movement.

Now that we have considered the historical significance of Mark's publication in light of other important dates in the first century CE, we return to the specific question of dating the Gospel. Since the text does not provide any clear information that would allow us to date the Gospel definitively, we are forced to rely on internal clues to propose a possible range of dates. It is widely thought that Mark 13—also known as "the little apocalypse"—situates Mark's Gospel around the time of the first Jewish war with Rome (66–74 CE). From the perspective of both Jews and early Christians, one of the most significant moments of that war was the Roman destruction of the Second Temple in the year 70 CE. At the beginning of Mark 13, one of Jesus's disciples comments on the grandeur of the temple: "Look, Teacher, what large stones and what large buildings!" To this Jesus responds, "Do you see these great buildings? Not one stone will be left here upon another; all will be thrown down" (Mark 13:1–2). Following this comment, Jesus sits opposite the temple on the Mount of Olives with Peter, James, John, and Andrew (13:3) and begins to instruct them about the destruction of the temple, the end of Jerusalem, and the return of the Son of Man (13:4–37). Given what we know historically about the razing of the temple and the destruction of Jerusalem, Mark's presentation of this conversation between Jesus and the disciples hardly seems coincidental. About this event, the Jewish historian Josephus writes,

> The army now ha[d] no victims either for slaughter or plunder, through lack of all objects on which to vent their rage . . . Caesar ordered the whole city and the temple to be razed to the ground . . . All the rest of the wall encompassing the city was so completely levelled to the ground as to leave future visitors to the spot no ground for believing that it had ever been inhabited. Such was the end to which the frenzy of revolutionaries brought Jerusalem, that splendid city of worldwide renown. (*Jewish War*, 7.1.1)[5]

---

5. Flavius Josephus, *The Jewish War*, Books 5–7, trans. Henry St. John Thackeray, LCL 210 (Cambridge: Harvard University Press, 1928), 307.

The discourse in Mark 13 is seen by many as corresponding to this description of Jerusalem's fall. The conversation that takes place between Jesus and his disciples likely reflects something that Mark knows has just happened (or will soon take place and thus anticipated). While not all scholars agree that Mark was written during this period, 68–70 CE has been the consensus position among scholars since at least the middle of the twentieth century, with many leaning firmly in the direction of a 70 CE date *after* the destruction of the temple. This hypothesis also appears to have the greatest explanatory power for questions that arise elsewhere in the narrative. For our purposes, I will take the position that Mark was written and disseminated shortly after the destruction of the Second Temple in 70 CE.

Who Wrote the Gospel of Mark?

As with the question of dating, there is no information within the Gospel that would allow us to identify its author directly. It is widely recognized that Mark, along with the other canonical Gospels, is anonymous, and that the text originally circulated without the heading, "Gospel of Mark."[6] However, this is not terribly problematic as the genre to which the gospels belong does not require an author to self-identify within the text itself. In fact, the impulse for Christian authors of gospel texts to identify themselves appears to have emerged in the early second century, and usually in the case of

---

6. Most of our extant Greek manuscripts include the phrase, *kata ton Markon* ("according to Mark") either at the beginning or end of the text, though a handful are anonymous. It is probably the case that gospel titles were added to manuscripts in the early second century as gospel collections began to circulate within the church and there arose a need to distinguish the gospel texts from one another.

pseudonymous texts like the Gospel of Thomas or the Gospel of Peter.[7]

Despite the lack of direct internal evidence, there is ample external testimony associating the name "Mark" with the authorship of this Gospel, especially from the second century.[8] The first writer to identify Mark as the author of a gospel was Papias, the bishop of Hierapolis. While we no longer have access to his five-volume work, *Exposition of the Sayings of the Lord* (ca. 110–140 CE), Papias is cited by the early church historian Eusebius of Caesarea in his *Ecclesiastical History* (ca. 300–315 CE). In a quotation provided by Eusebius, Papias identifies Mark as both the author of the Gospel and as the "interpreter" of Peter:

> Mark became Peter's interpreter and wrote accurately all that he remembered, not, indeed, in order, of the things said or done by the Lord. For he had not heard the Lord, nor had he followed him, but later on, as I said, followed Peter, who used to give teaching as necessity demanded but not making, as it were, an arrangement of the Lord's oracles, so that Mark did nothing wrong in thus writing down single points as he remembered them. For to one thing he gave attention, to leave out nothing of what he heard and to make no false statements in them. (3.39.15)[9]

---

7. The Gospel of Thomas begins by identifying its author as "Didymus Judas Thomas," a disciple known to us previously only from the Gospel of John. Similarly, the Gospel of Peter identifies its author as "Simon Peter, the brother of Andrew," whom we know from the four canonical Gospels. There is no evidence to support these authorial claims and scholars unanimously regard these texts as pseudonymous.

8. One of the most enigmatic suggestions scholars have posed has been the claim that the naked young man who flees in Gethsemane (14:51–52) should be understood as a veiled reference to the author, who is also an eyewitness.

9. Eusebius, *Ecclesiastical History*, Book 11, trans. Kirsopp Lake, LCL 153 (Cambridge: Harvard University Press, 1926), 297.

According to Papias then, Peter did not intend to give a full account of Jesus's ministry but delivered his message in piecemeal as the occasion demanded; Mark simply wrote to the best of his remembrance, even though he ultimately provided an incomplete account. Despite the antiquity of this citation, we need to be cautious in accepting some of the details of Papias's testimony as there are clear problems with his historical reporting, not just here, but elsewhere.[10]

In addition to Papias, other early Christian writers including Irenaeus (ca. 180 CE), Clement of Alexandria (ca. 185–190 CE), Tertullian (ca. 207 CE), and Origen (ca. 200–250 CE) all make some reference to Mark's authorship of this text. While it may be the case that these writers were relying on a common tradition rather than independently attesting to Mark's authorial role, there are still good reasons to think that a Christian named Mark composed the text. First, though the name Mark was popular within the Roman Empire at this time, there are not many figures known to us by that name in the NT. In fact, none of the figures in the immediate circles of Jesus seems to have gone by that name. Therefore, if one were attributing an unknown gospel to an early Christian figure, it would make much more sense to link the authorship of that text to an authoritative individual within early Christian circles. On this issue, Joel Marcus comments:

> [T]here is only one Mark known to us from early church history, a rather minor associate of Paul who is mentioned in Acts and the Pauline correspondence. The relative

---

10. Perhaps the most conspicuous example of questionable reporting on Papias's part is his suggestion—appearing a bit later in the passage excerpted here—that Matthew's text was originally composed in "the Hebrew language" (= Aramaic) and subsequently translated into Greek. Scholars nearly unanimously reject this idea.

insignificance of this person is one reason for thinking that the Gospel was actually written by a Mark; if, lacking a sure tradition of authorship, a scribe had wished to ascribe an anonymous Gospel fictionally to a church hero, he would have chosen a more illustrious name, probably that of one of Jesus' twelve disciples.[11]

Our best evidence suggests that the early church was interested in safeguarding its chosen texts as both truthful and authoritative, and one way of accomplishing this was to establish clear authorial connections to those in the inner circles of Jesus.[12] In light of this move to connect the authorship of early Christian texts to important figures, Marcus's point is well-taken. If we adopt the view that a Christian named Mark was responsible for the authorship of this Gospel, we are left with two related questions: (1) Which "Mark" are we talking about? and (2) Is it possible for us to know with any degree of certainty?

As mentioned above, there are not many figures named Mark in the NT, and the two figures who go by that name have traditionally been treated by interpreters as being one and the same. In Acts 12, we briefly meet a figure named "John, also called Mark" (commonly shortened to John Mark) who accompanies Paul and Barnabas on their first missionary journey (Acts 12:25) but ends up abandoning them before the

---

11. Joel Marcus, *Mark 1–8: A New Translation with Introduction and Commentary*, AB 27 (New York: Doubleday, 2000), 18.

12. We must recognize an apologetic impulse within the early church as it relates to identifying scriptural texts. Early in the process that led to canonization, each of the four Gospels was explicitly connected to an authoritative figure. The Gospels of Matthew and John were ascribed to disciples of Jesus. Luke was identified as an associate of Paul, and Mark was identified as both a companion of Paul *and* the interpreter of Peter. Whether all these claims are accurate or not—and we cannot really know for certain—these moves were clearly an attempt by the early church to safeguard the authority of these texts by establishing the apostolic credentials of each author.

trip is complete (Acts 13:13; cf. Acts 15:38–39). According to Acts, a dispute over whether to bring John Mark on a subsequent journey is ultimately the reason for Paul and Barnabas parting ways as missionary companions (Acts 15:36–41).

The name Mark also appears several times in the Pauline correspondence. In Philemon 24, a Mark is listed among Paul's fellow workers. In 2 Timothy 4:11, a Mark is described as "useful" to Paul. Perhaps most significantly for this developing picture, Colossians 4:10 names "Mark, the cousin of Barnabas" as among Paul's companions. An additional reference to an individual named Mark is found outside the Pauline correspondence in 1 Peter 5:13, but in the same context as a reference to Silas (1 Pet 5:12), another individual consistently connected to Paul in the NT (cf. Acts 15–18; 1 Thess 1:1; 2 Thess 1:1; 2 Cor 1:19). This evidence has led scholars to conclude that the John Mark of Acts is the same Mark mentioned in the Pauline letters and 1 Peter.

However, even if we accept that the John Mark of Acts is the same Mark associated with Paul and Peter, we are still no closer to determining whether this particular Mark was responsible for writing the Gospel. While some scholars have made attempts to be more definitive about the identity of our author, to say much more is to risk going further than the evidence will allow. For our purposes here I accept that the Gospel was composed by a first-century Christian named Mark. We must remain circumspect about the rest.

WHERE AND FOR WHOM WAS THE GOSPEL WRITTEN?

When we consider the question of Mark's earliest audience, we are asking at least two related questions: "*Where* was the Gospel written?" and "*Who* was the intended audience of the

Gospel?" As with the questions we have considered thus far, we are forced to rely on external testimony and a certain degree of historical reconstruction as there are no explicit answers to these questions within the text of Mark.

The most common conclusion offered by scholars has been that the Gospel of Mark was written in Rome. This view has a long history in NT scholarship and is rooted in the testimony of Clement of Alexandria (ca 185–190 CE), recounted here by Eusebius (ca 300–315 CE):

> And again in the same books Clement has inserted a tradition of the primitive elders with regard to the order of the Gospels, as follows. He said that those Gospels were first written which include the genealogies, but that the Gospel according to Mark came into being in this manner: When Peter had publicly preached the word at Rome, and by the Spirit had proclaimed the Gospel, that those present, who were many, exhorted Mark, as one who had followed him for a long time and remembered what had been spoken, to make a record of what was said; and that he did this, and distributed the Gospel among those that asked him. (*Ecclesiastical History*, 6.14.5–6)[13]

In addition to Clement's testimony, commentators have often pointed to Mark's use of Latin loanwords and Latinisms, along with his seemingly inadequate knowledge of Palestinian geography, as indicators that the Gospel was composed in Rome.[14]

---

13. Eusebius, *Ecclesiastical History*, Books 6–10, trans. J. E. L. Oulton, LCL 265 (Cambridge: Harvard University Press, 1932), 47–49.

14. These include *modius* (4:21), *legio* (5:9, 15), *speculator* (6:27), *sextarius* (7:4), *census* (12:14), *denarius* (12:15), *quadrans* (12:42), *flagellum* (15:15), *praetorium* (15:16), and *centurio* (15:39, 44, 45).

Despite recent challenges to this theory, Mark's Roman provenance remains a standard position among scholars.

It has not been common among interpreters to argue that Mark was composed in Alexandria, though the early Christian writer John Chrysostom is a notable exception. Discussing Matthew's supposed Alexandrian provenance, Chrysostom writes, "And Mark too, in Egypt, is said to have done this self-same thing at the entreaty of the disciples" (*Homilies on the Gospel of Matthew*, 1.7).[15] However, this is most likely a misreading of Eusebius's testimony that seems to indicate that Mark *first* wrote his Gospel and *then* went to Alexandria: "They say that this Mark was the first to be sent to preach in Egypt the Gospel which he had also put into writing, and was the first to establish churches in Alexandria itself" (*Ecclesiastical History*, 2.16.1).[16] While this citation likely has little bearing on our attempts to identify the Gospel's *provenance*, it does tell us something about the *early dissemination of the Gospel*, which we will discuss in greater detail below.

A small minority has insisted that Mark was composed in Galilee, but that view has failed to gain a wide following. Over the past two decades, Syria has become the chief alternative to the view that Mark was composed in Rome. Some scholars have advanced the view that Mark was written in Syrian Antioch, while others have argued for its composition in southern Syria. Advocates of this position are quick to object that the only real evidence we have for a Roman provenance is the connection Papias draws between Mark and Peter, and this is not exactly certain. They also dispute the importance of Latinisms and Latin loanwords as being a definite

---

15. John Chrysostom, *St. Chrysostom: Homilies on the Gospel of Saint Matthew*, in *A Select Library of the Nicene and Post-Nicene Fathers of the Christian Church*, ed. Philip Schaff, vol. 10 (Grand Rapids: Eerdmans, 1956), 3–4.

16. Eusebius, *Ecclesiastical History*, Books 1–5, 145.

indicator of the Gospel's connection to Rome. Most of these loanwords are connected in some way to the Roman military, and they would just as easily make sense to those within a territory under Roman occupation. Perhaps the most important scholar to advocate for this position in recent years has been Joel Marcus, who situates the writing of the Gospel during the first Jewish war with Rome (66–74 CE) and sees the destruction of the temple as the catalyst for Mark's composition, all of which is reflected in Mark 13 (as discussed above). Against that backdrop, Marcus notes that: (1) Syria was close enough to Palestine—where the events of Jesus's ministry occurred—that there would have been relatively close contact with traditions about Jesus reflected in the Gospel, (2) Syria was predominantly a gentile region influenced by the preaching of Paul, and this would help account for Mark's emphasis on issues like freedom from the law, Jesus's relationship with non-Jews, and the consistent explanation of Aramaic terms (5:41; 7:11, 34; 15:34) and Jewish religious customs (7:3–4; 14:12; 15:42), and (3) the instruction to Judean Christians to "flee to the mountains" at the appearance of the "abomination that causes desolation" (13:14–15 NIV) probably reflects the experience of Mark's community; the "hills" in question are likely on the eastern edge of the Jordan Valley. This location corresponds to early testimonies by Eusebius (ca. 300–315 CE) and Epiphanius (ca. 374–375 CE) about the flight of Judean Christians to Syria during persecution, after which the conflict in Palestine ultimately spilled over into Syria.[17] Marcus's reconstruction is complex and incorporates factors not considered by previous theories. While still a minority position, the Syrian view of Mark's provenance continues to gain momentum among scholars.

---

17. See the full discussion in Marcus, *Mark 1–8*, 33–37.

We see that the history of scholarship has variously suggested that Mark was written in Rome, Alexandria, Galilee, Syrian Antioch, and southern Syria.[18] With all those options in mind, it is worth noting that we do not know for certain where any of our NT texts were written and these questions remain matters of serious discussion in contemporary NT scholarship. Scholars on all sides of the debate make points worthy of serious consideration and as with the questions we have already considered, a sense of certainty remains elusive. I find most persuasive the view that Mark was written somewhere in Syria, and that is the position I will adopt here.

The second question we need to consider is, "Who was the intended audience of the Gospel?" In the current landscape, this question is fraught with a bit more difficulty than the issue of Mark's provenance. Against the backdrop of contemporary gospel scholarship, a more specific version of this question might be, "Was Mark writing for a specific community, or did Mark write his Gospel with the purpose of disseminating it throughout the Roman world?" Since the early twentieth century, gospel scholarship has operated under the nearly unquestioned assumption that the Gospels were written for individual communities, churches, or groups of churches. This assumption—which emerged during the eras dominated by form criticism and redaction criticism—reigned as one of the assured results of modern gospel scholarship until the late twentieth century. In 1998, Richard Bauckham published an

---

18. During the formation of the earliest Christian churches, the three largest and most influential cities within the Roman Empire were (in order): Rome, Alexandria, and Syrian Antioch. These three cities ultimately became major centers of Christian activity. Among those writings not composed in Greek, the majority of early Christian writings and NT manuscripts in the first five centuries CE were composed in Latin, Coptic, and Syriac—the three languages other than Greek associated with these major urban centers. It is therefore not surprising that these three cities often appear as suggestions for the locales in which NT texts were produced.

influential book, *Gospels for All Christians*, which represented the first substantial challenge to the "gospel communities" hypothesis.[19]

Scholars involved in reconstructing gospel communities tended to be skeptical about the historical quality of the material narrated in the Gospels. One consequence of this approach was to reject the historicity of much of the content of the Gospels, while creating and defending—often with conviction—a historical reconstruction of the community's evolution, religious convictions, and inner conflicts. And a further byproduct of this approach was the habit of reading the Gospels not as narratives about Jesus, but rather as narratives about reconstructed hypothetical communities standing behind the texts themselves. While Bauckham's criticism of this trend was valid and demonstrated a need for a nuanced corrective, there remains debate over the question of whether the Gospel writers intended their narratives, first and foremost, for specific communities.

Bauckham begins with the assertion—which I accept—that all four Gospels were intended for Christian audiences, as opposed to being written for the purpose of evangelizing non-Christian audiences. He goes on to argue: (1) that unlike the letters of Paul, which are clearly addressed to individual communities, the Gospels are examples of Greco-Roman biographies and thus presumed a much wider readership, (2) the early Christian movement is not just a group of isolated and independent churches but a cohesive network of churches that kept in fairly close contact with one another, (3) the earliest churches saw themselves as part of a worldwide movement,

---

19. Richard Bauckham, ed., *The Gospels for All Christians: Rethinking the Gospel Audiences* (Grand Rapids: Eerdmans, 1998). While the book is an edited collection, there is little doubt that Bauckham's opening chapter, "For Whom Were the Gospels Written?" proved to be the most influential.

and (4) even if they existed, the gospel communities ultimately have no real hermeneutical bearing on our interpretation of the Gospels. Responses to Bauckham's thesis were mixed but equally effusive in both directions, and the ripple effects of his argument can still be felt today. It is safe to say that a large segment of gospel scholarship remains skeptical of his conclusions.[20]

While it is true that some of the community reconstructions of the mid-to-late twentieth century were too speculative, there is little doubt that those responsible for writing the Gospels were members of social networks. Those networks shaped and informed their understanding of Jesus, his ministry, and its significance for their immediate circumstances. Bauckham is correct that the Gospels were widely disseminated early after their composition, but it does not naturally follow that they therefore were intended for all Christians. It is possible for the Gospels to have been written for and within a specific social network *and* for them to have been widely distributed to Christian communities. Throughout the remainder of this book, I accept that the Gospel of Mark was likely intended to address the concerns of a specific social network of Christians in Syria while also being disseminated to Christian communities throughout the Roman Empire. An important part of the literary

---

20. For critical engagement with Bauckham's thesis on both sides of the debate, see David C. Sim, "The Gospels for All Christians? A Response to Richard Bauckham," *JSNT* 24.2 (2001): 3–27; Philip F. Esler, "Community and Gospel in Early Christianity: A Response to Richard Bauckham's *Gospels for All Christians*," *SJT* 51.2 (1998): 235–48; and Margaret M. Mitchell, "Patristic Counter-Evidence to the Claim That 'The Gospels Were Written for All Christians,'" *NTS* 51.1 (2005): 36–79. *The Audience of the Gospels: The Origin and Function of the Gospels in Early Christianity*, ed. Edward W. Klink III, LNTS 353 (London: T&T Clark, 2010) contains several helpful responses to Bauckham's thesis. Noteworthy among these is the chapter by Craig Blomberg, "The Gospels for Specific Communities and All Christians," 111–33.

strategy employed later in the book will proceed from these conclusions.

What Is Mark Trying to Accomplish with This Story?

The gospel narratives are not objective historical treatises. They are religious texts aimed at persuasion. A text with this type of rhetorical aim is slanted in such a way as to cause an audience to embrace its perspective. This is how the Gospels operate—each has a specific perspective on the life and ministry of Jesus, and each wants the narrative to demonstrate this perspective with its own rhetoric of persuasion. With this in mind, it is important to recognize that Mark has a clear agenda for his audience and that he wants to persuade the audience to embrace his vision of Jesus. To illustrate: note that Mark does not write, "Dear audience, here is some objective information about things that Jesus said and did. Please read this text and make up your own minds about him." On the contrary, Mark begins his narrative by identifying Jesus as "Christ, the Son of God" (1:1).[21] Mark's Jesus does not meet some of the traditional expectations of a Jewish Messiah, nor does he appear to rival Caesar as "Son of God"—a title central to Roman imperial propaganda. In fact, Mark's Jesus loses his life at the hands of the very people a Messiah is expected to conquer. Mark proceeds to use the remainder of his narrative as a vehicle for demonstrating both *how* and *why* Jesus is the Christ and Son of God.

But understanding this is not an easy task. Mark's Jesus tries to silence those who would preach about him publicly. Does he not want people to spread the word? Mark's Jesus tells his disciples that he speaks in parables with the express goal of *concealing his message* from the masses. Does he not want

---

21. Mark's Christological portrait will be the focus of chapters 3 and 4.

the crowds to turn to God? Mark's Jesus does other puzzling things. For example, he allows a legion of demons to occupy a herd of swine and insults a woman who comes to him for help with her suffering child. Should he not behave differently? Mark wants to show us his picture of Jesus, but we can only appreciate his vision by abandoning our preconceived notions and allowing this distinctive portrait to emerge. What is Mark trying to accomplish with this story of Jesus? I suggest he wants to upend the foundation of his readers' supposed knowledge about what a "Christ" and "Son of God" should be in first-century Roman Palestine and force us to ponder, "How are we to reckon with a *crucified* Christ and Son of God?"

With that in mind, the approach undertaken throughout the remainder of this book is a historically informed, close reading of the distinctive literary and theological features of Mark's Gospel as it exists in its final form. This approach has been labeled, "narrative criticism," and it has manifested itself in various iterations over the past four decades.[22] In short, we begin with the assumption that the Gospel of Mark reached its final form—or at least the final form that has come down to us (1:1–16:8)—for numerous reasons. Among those reasons is that it was regarded as a coherent and meaningful story in its own right. Thus, the final form of Mark's Gospel possesses unity, internal coherence, and many of the features that readers would expect from such a narrative: a plot that progressively develops, important spatial and situational settings, the positioning and use of major and minor characters, and motifs that work at both the literary and theological levels. In other words, irrespective of source and form-critical concerns

---

22. For a helpful primer on narrative criticism and the related approaches it has spawned, see Patricia K. Tull, "Narrative Criticism and Narrative Hermeneutics," in *The Oxford Encyclopedia of Biblical Interpretation*, ed. Steven L. McKenzie (Oxford: Oxford University Press, 2013), 37–46.

that lie behind the text and might be the concern of other interpreters, we are concerned here primarily with *the world of the text* as it exists in its final form.[23] Our goal in this book is to uncover what makes this treatment of Jesus unique and to trace the narrative rhetoric as it unfolds in Mark's telling of the story. Such an approach to the themes of the narrative will provide us with the tools to better answer the question, "What is Mark trying to accomplish with this story of Jesus?"

A FINAL WORD: LET MARK BE MARK

While not true for everyone, many readers come to the NT with what I describe as a "Jesus-mosaic" in mind. Perhaps they have read portions of the Bible or in some cases, the entire book. Often, they have been exposed to Bible studies and all different varieties of preaching and teaching. In some cases, they may have even read widely outside the NT on issues related to biblical interpretation. All this learning, while useful, leads to a specific type of understanding: Jesus becomes the byproduct of robust theological formulations informed by centuries of Christian reflection. However, this approach to reading the NT has the potential to rob readers of their ability to see the unique presentation of Jesus set forth in each individual text, whether a Gospel or one of the epistles.

There is no single NT writing that presents Jesus as the fully developed subject that has resulted from two millennia of Christian theological reflection. Each NT text provides us with a "snapshot," a unique and distinctive portrait that begs to be taken seriously on its own terms. This means that

---

23. We will discuss the assumptions and goals of narrative criticism in greater detail in chapter 2.

we must do our best to read each NT text as its own fully autonomous writing, with a unique point of view and rhetoric of persuasion before we attempt to place those texts into conversation with one another. Thus, when we read the Gospel of Mark, we must resist the urge to conflate the various portraits of Jesus and construct our own "Jesus-mosaic," at least for the time being.

To illustrate this further, the Gospel of John presents Jesus as a divine *Logos* from the very beginning of the narrative (John 1:1). Not only does Mark not do this, but such a description never appears to be part of Mark's narrative or theological agenda. In fact, much of the specific language and imagery that are unique to John's vision of Jesus are missing from Mark. By contrast, Mark's understanding of Jesus has its own shape, imagery, and terminology, and is markedly different in places from the presentation of Jesus in the other three canonical Gospels. It would be a mistake, then, to assume a fully divine Jesus when reading Mark's Gospel, because that element is simply missing from his narrative.[24] The same could and should be said for both Matthew and Luke, even though each tells their story of Jesus in a distinctive way.[25]

Similarly, the Gospels of Matthew and Luke narrate miraculous circumstances surrounding the conception and birth

---

24. To be fair, others are persuaded that Mark's Christology is much closer to the sort of presentation we see in the Fourth Gospel, Colossians, or Hebrews. For a recent presentation of diverse views on the subject, see Anthony Le Donne, ed., *Christology in Mark's Gospel: Four Views* (Grand Rapids: Zondervan Academic, 2021).

25. It is also important to read the NT apart from later creedal and confessional developments. Confessions like the Nicene Creed (325 CE) and Chalcedonian Definition (451 CE) were critical to the development of orthodox Christian theology, and they are the result of centuries of reflection, controversy, and debate. However, there is no one-to-one correspondence between any first-century Christian text and these later, more developed dogmas.

of Jesus (Matt 1:18–24; Luke 1:26–38; 2:1–21). By contrast,
Mark's story begins with an adult Jesus who is immediately
baptized by John the Baptist and cast out into the wilderness
(1:9–13). It would likewise be a mistake to read Mark's text
by appealing to information about Jesus's birth that has not
been narrated by Mark.

It is critical for us to read each NT writing on its own
terms. Simply stated, we must let Mark be Mark. We must
attempt to read the Gospel in light of its own literary distinc-
tives and theological emphases. Only then will we be able to
appreciate his specific contribution(s) to our understanding
of Jesus. Throughout the remainder of this book, we will look
at the distinctive features of Mark's Gospel, seeking to dis-
cover what is unique to his presentation of the life, teaching,
ministry, death, and resurrection of Jesus. Only after we have
appreciated Mark's unique christological vision, and the way
that vision challenges its readers, can we then ask how this
Gospel fits with the remaining NT portraits of Jesus.

FOR FURTHER READING

A. Nontechnical Treatments of Introductory Issues in Mark's Gospel

Achtemeier, Paul, Joel B. Green, and Marianne Meye Thompson.
    "The Gospel According to Mark." In *Introducing the New
    Testament: Its Literature and Theology*, 123–48. Grand Rapids:
    Eerdmans, 2001.
Johnson, Luke Timothy. "The Gospel of Mark." In *The Writings
    of the New Testament: An Interpretation*, 143–64. 3rd ed.
    Minneapolis: Fortress, 2010.
Powell, Mark Allan. "Mark." In *Introducing the New Testament: A
    Historical, Literary, and Theological Survey*, 141–59. 2nd ed.
    Grand Rapids: Baker Academic, 2018.

B. Advanced/Technical Treatments of Introductory Issues in Mark's Gospel

Garland, David E. "The Orientation of This Study and the Historical Framework for Mark's Theology." In *A Theology of Mark's Gospel*. Biblical Theology of the New Testament, 39–98. Grand Rapids: Zondervan Academic, 2015.

Marcus, Joel. "Introduction." In *Mark 1–8: A New Translation with Introduction and Commentary*, 15–79. AB 27. New York: Doubleday, 2000.

Yarbro Collins, Adela. "Introduction." In *Mark*, 1–119. Hermeneia. Minneapolis: Fortress, 2007.

C. Situating Mark Against Its Historical, Social, and Religious Backgrounds

Blackwell, Ben C., John K. Goodrich, and Jason Maston, eds. *Reading Mark in Context: Jesus in Second Temple Judaism*. Grand Rapids: Zondervan Academic, 2018.

D. Gospel Genre

Becker, Eve-Marie. *The Birth of Christian History: Memory and Time from Mark to Luke-Acts*. AYBRL. New Haven: Yale University Press, 2017.

Bond, Helen. *The First Biography of Jesus: Genre and Meaning in Mark's Gospel*. Grand Rapids: Eerdmans, 2020.

Burridge, Richard. *What Are the Gospels? A Comparison with Graeco-Roman Biography*. 25th anniv. ed. Waco, TX: Baylor University Press, 2020.

Capes, David B. "*Imitatio Christi* and the Gospel Genre." *BBR* 13.1 (2003): 1–19.

Smith, Justin M. *Why Bíos? On the Relationship Between Gospel Genre and Implied Audience*. LNTS 518. London: Bloomsbury/T&T Clark, 2015.

Yarbro Collins, Adela. "Genre and the Gospels." *JR* 75.2 (1995): 239–46.

E. Narrative Readings of Mark

Dewey, Joanna, David Rhoads, and Donald Michie. *Mark as Story: An Introduction to the Narrative of a Gospel.* 3rd. ed. Minneapolis: Fortress, 2012.

Fowler, Robert M. *Let the Reader Understand: Reader-Response Criticism and the Gospel of Mark.* Minneapolis: Fortress, 1991.

Iverson, Kelly R. *Reading Mark.* Cascade Companions. Eugene, OR: Cascade, 2023.

Juel, Donald. *A Master of Surprise: Mark Interpreted.* Minneapolis: Fortress, 2002.

Kingsbury, Jack Dean, *Conflict in Mark: Jesus, Authorities, Disciples.* Minneapolis: Fortress, 1989.

AN OUTLINE OF MARK'S GOSPEL

I.   Prologue (1:1–15)

II. Who is this man? (1:16–8:30)

    A. Early ministry (1:16–45)

        1. Jesus calls his first disciples by the sea (1:16–20)

        2. Jesus ministers in Capernaum: exorcism, healing, preaching (1:21–39)

        3. Jesus cleanses a leper (1:40–45)

    B. Ministry and conflict in Galilee (2:1–3:12)

        1. Jesus heals a paralytic in Capernaum (2:1–12)

        2. Jesus calls Levi by the lake (2:13–17)

        3. Jesus questioned about fasting (2:18–22)

        4. Controversy over plucking heads of grain on the Sabbath (2:23–28)

        5. Jesus restores a withered hand in a synagogue (3:1–6)

        6. Crowds follow Jesus around the lake (3:7–12)

    C. On a mountain, all around the lake, and in Jesus's hometown (3:13–6:6a)

        1. Jesus appoints the Twelve on a mountain (3:13–19)

        2. Jesus's family, his accusers, and the creation a "new family" (3:20–35) [Mark's first "sandwich" passage][26]

        3. Jesus preaches the parable of the sower by the lake (4:1–20) [Mark's second "sandwich" passage]

---

26. Mark's use of intercalation or "sandwiching" will be discussed in chapter 5.

4. Jesus preaches other parables by the lake
    (4:21–34)
5. Jesus calms a storm on the lake (4:35–41)
6. Jesus exorcises a "Legion" on the "other"
    side of the lake (5:1–20)
7. Jesus, Jairus, and a nameless woman on the
    Jewish side of the lake (5:21–43) [Mark's
    third "sandwich" passage]
8. Jesus rejected in his hometown (6:1–6a)

D. Ministry in Bethsaida, Tyre, Sidon, the
   Decapolis, Dalmanutha, and Caesarea Philippi
   (6:6b–8:30)

1. Jesus, Herod, John the Baptist, and the
    Twelve (6:6b–31) [Mark's fourth "sandwich"
    passage]
2. Jesus feeds five thousand in a desolate place
    (6:32–44)
3. Jesus walks on the sea (6:45–56)
4. Jesus is challenged and questioned by the
    Pharisees (7:1–16)
5. Jesus takes his disciples aside (7:17–23)
6. Jesus and a Syrophoenician woman in Tyre
    (7:24–30)
7. Jesus heals a deaf and mute man in Sidon
    (7:31–37)
8. Jesus feeds four thousand in a remote place
    (8:1–8)
9. Jesus and the disciples in Dalmanutha
    (8:9–13)
10. Jesus warns his disciples about the Pharisees
    and Herod (8:14–21)
11. Jesus heals a blind man at Bethsaida
    (8:22–26)

---

27. There is an ongoing debate about what represents the so-called "turning point" in Mark's Gospel. It is generally recognized that there is a pivot around 8:27–30. For an intriguing proposal that sees this passage as having a "Janus effect" (i.e., looking backward and forward at the same time), see Gregg S. Morrison, *The Turning Point in the Gospel of Mark: A Study in Markan Christology* (Eugene, OR: Pickwick, 2014).

1. Jesus hailed as king during his triumphal entry (11:1–11)
2. Jesus, the fig tree, and the temple: an enacted parable (11:12–25) [Mark's fifth "sandwich" passage]
3. Chief priests, scribes, and elders question Jesus (11:27–12:12)
4. Pharisees and Herodians question Jesus (12:13–17)
5. Sadducees question Jesus (12:18–27)
6. A teacher of the law questions Jesus (12:28–34)
7. Jesus teaches in the temple (12:35–44)
8. Jesus sits on the Mount of Olives opposite the temple and predicts the destruction of the temple, the end of Jerusalem, and the return of the Son of Man (13:1–37)

C. The passion, death, and burial in Jerusalem (14:1–15:47)

1. Jesus anointed at Bethany (14:1–11) [Mark's sixth "sandwich" passage]
2. Jesus celebrates a Passover meal with the disciples (14:12–26)
3. Jesus predicts Peter's denial (14:27–31)
4. Jesus prays and is arrested in Gethsemane (14:32–52)
5. The Sanhedrin condemns Jesus, and Peter denies him (14:53–72) [Mark's seventh "sandwich" passage]
6. Pilate talks with Jesus, flogs him, and hands him over for crucifixion (15:1–20)
7. Jesus is crucified at Golgotha (15:21–41)

    8. Jesus is buried in a tomb cut out of rock
       (15:42–47)

IV. Conclusion: Resurrection? (16:1–8)[28]

---

28. There is no little debate surrounding the various endings of Mark. While the majority of manuscripts contain the so-called longer ending, which consists of 16:9–20, most contemporary scholars accept that the Gospel ends at 16:8. For a helpful overview of the various endings and scholarly opinion surrounding them, see Kelly R. Iverson, *Reading Mark*, Cascade Companions (Eugene, OR: Cascade, 2023), 146–74.

CHAPTER 2

The Reception of Mark and the Development of Christian Theology

B efore we can enter a discussion of major themes in Mark, it will prove important first to understand how the Gospel has informed and contributed to developments within Christian theology. As briefly stated in the previous chapter, in comparison to other biblical texts, Mark was seemingly overlooked for centuries in favor of writings that were deemed more preferable for the developing theological teachings of the church. Mark was clearly overshadowed by Matthew, which was the favored Gospel for the earliest Christian lectionaries, going back to the second century. With its three references to the "church," all on the lips of Jesus (16:18; 18:17 [2x]), Matthew also became known as the "the Gospel of the Church" from an early period. This, along with Jesus's five discourses, cemented Matthew's importance for early Christian doctrinal and ethical formulations.[1]

---

1. Scholars recognize that Matthew's Gospel is structured around five major discourses of Jesus: (1) the Sermon on the Mount (5:1–7:29), (2) the Missionary Discourse (10:1–42), (3) the Discourse in Parables (13:1–58), (4) the Ecclesiological Discourse (18:1–35), and (5) the Eschatological Discourse (24:1–25:46). These discourses contain most of the ethical teaching found in Matthew.

The Gospel of John was also widely influential across the various iterations of earliest Christianity. Clear evidence of this early influence is that the first two commentaries we have for any of the canonical Gospels were written on the Gospel of John. Both were penned in the second century by Valentinian Gnostics, the first by Ptolemy (ca. 140–160 CE) and the second by Heracleon (ca. 170 CE).[2] By contrast, the earliest commentary on Mark's Gospel did not appear until the seventh century CE,[3] and even after that, commentaries on Mark remained a relative rarity. Further, John's emphasis on the unique relationship between Jesus and the God of Israel (e.g., John 1:1; 8:58; 10:30) was foundational for what ultimately became orthodox Christology. It is doubtful whether the church fathers could have arrived at a doctrinal formulation like that established at the Council of Chalcedon without the presence of the Fourth Gospel. Even today one can easily discern the influence of John's Gospel on various trajectories within Christian theology.

When we move away from the Gospels, we also see the influence of other NT texts for early developments in Christian doctrine and self-understanding. The Acts of the Apostles provided the church with its first history of the nascent Jesus movement, and Paul's letters, especially Romans, 1 Corinthians, and Galatians, had a significant impact on the shape of important doctrines such as justification, original sin, resurrection, and the various understandings of the atonement. Each of these texts offered something foundational

---

2. On this, see Elaine Pagels, *The Johannine Gospel in Gnostic Exegesis: Heracleon's Commentary on John*, SBLMS 17 (Nashville: Abingdon, 1973).

3. See the discussion in Michael Cahill, *The First Commentary on Mark: An Annotated Translation* (Oxford: Oxford University Press, 1998), 3–4. The earliest patristic writing on Mark was written by Victor of Antioch (late fifth century CE), but the work reads less like a commentary and more like a catena of texts drawn directly from the Gospel.

for earliest attempts to organize and systematize Christian thought. Against the backdrop of these important theological developments, Mark apparently was judged as having less to contribute, and the inattention to his Gospel persisted for centuries.

However, in the late eighteenth century, Mark's Gospel finally began coming into its own as scholars recognized its importance to the development of the gospel tradition. Not only did scholars establish that Mark was likely the earliest written text to narrate the life and ministry of Jesus, but they also realized that both Matthew and Luke (and possibly John) made substantial use of Mark's text when creating their own narratives about Jesus.[4] Since these revelations have become a foundational component of our understanding of gospel origins, Mark has been at the forefront of many important discussions in gospels research for nearly 250 years. While we cannot trace a history of influence for Mark that is as wide or deep as that of some other NT writings, we can shine a light on important methodological developments within gospel studies over the past two-and-a-half centuries. These developments have set the stage for the modern study of the

---

4. John's familiarity with the Synoptic Gospels is still a subject of serious debate among NT scholars. On this question, James Barker notes that nearly 1,900 years of writing on the subject has produced several periods of "consensus"—including John's complete independence from the Synoptics, John's knowledge of all three Synoptics, and various iterations of the latter position. Scholars are still sharply divided on the question. For more on this, see James W. Barker, *John's Use of Matthew*, Emerging Scholars (Minneapolis: Fortress, 2015), 1–14. For various angles on the idea that John was familiar with or dependent on Mark, see the excellent collection of essays in Eve-Marie Becker, Helen K. Bond, Catrin H. Williams, eds., *John's Transformation of Mark* (London: T&T Clark, 2021). Two excellent forthcoming books are poised to usher in a new consensus on the question of John's knowledge of the Synoptics; see James W. Barker, *Writing and Rewriting the Gospels: John and the Synoptics* (Grand Rapids: Eerdmans, 2025), and Mark Goodacre, *The Fourth Synoptic Gospel: John's Knowledge of Matthew, Mark, and Luke* (Grand Rapids: Eerdmans, 2025).

gospel tradition—a space in which there is no denying Mark's importance.

MARK AND METHODOLOGICAL DEVELOPMENTS

Establishing Markan Priority

The longstanding question about the relationship between the three Synoptic Gospels—Mark, Matthew, and Luke—has come to be known as the Synoptic problem. This problem represents a significant discussion within NT studies and is important for our understanding of various Christian doctrines.[5] In their writings on the composition of the four canonical Gospels, the church fathers nearly unanimously supported the idea that Matthew was the first of the Gospels to appear. We call this idea "Matthean priority." This tradition was supported by numerous important figures, including Papias (ca. 95–110 CE), Irenaeus (ca. 180 CE), Clement of Alexandria (ca. 185–190 CE), Origen (ca. 245–250 CE), Eusebius (ca. 320 CE), and Jerome (398 CE). The view was further cemented after Augustine published his important *Harmony of the Gospels* (ca. 400 CE), in which he wrote the following about the ordering of our Gospel texts:

> Now, those four evangelists whose names have gained the most remarkable circulation over the whole world, and whose number has been fixed as four . . . are believed to

---

5. The Synoptic problem has implications for numerous areas of research, one of which is challenging earlier understandings of verbal inspiration.

have written in the order which follows: first Matthew, then
Mark, thirdly Luke, lastly John. (1.2.3)[6]

And regarding Mark's role he asserts:

Mark follows him [i.e., Matthew] closely, and looks like his
attendant and epitomizer . . . For in his narrative he gives
nothing in concert with John apart from the others: by
himself separately, he has little to record; in conjunction
with Luke, as distinguished from the rest, he has still less;
but in concord with Matthew, he has a very large number
of passages. (1.2.4)[7]

So great was Augustine's influence that the canonical ordering of the NT is said to have resulted from his exposition of
the ordering of the Gospels. His view of synoptic relations is
known today as the Augustinian hypothesis, which a majority
of scholars no longer consider a viable explanation for the
Synoptic problem, though it long reigned supreme.

The idea of Matthean Priority persisted in scholarship
on the Gospels until the rise of higher criticism within the
German academy. In 1786, a German scholar named Gottlob
Christian Storr was the first to argue for Markan priority,[8]
though his view gained little momentum until it was picked
up by later and more influential scholars. Others whose work
was foundational for establishing Markan priority include the
German scholars Karl Lachmann (1835) and H. J. Holtzmann

---

6. Augustine, *St. Augustine: Harmony of the Gospels,* in *Nicene and Post-Nicene
Fathers: First Series,* ed. Philip Schaff, trans. S. D. F. Salmond, vol. 6 (Buffalo:
Christian Literature Publishing Co., 1888), 79.

7. Augustine, *St. Augustine: Harmony of the Gospels,* 79.

8. Gottlob Christian Storr, *Über den Zweck der evangelischen Geschichte und
der Briefe Johannis* (Tübingen: Hörbrandt, 1786). [An English translation of the
German title: *On the Purpose of the Gospel History and the Letters of John.*]

(1863), and the British scholars F. C. Burkitt (1906), and B. H. Streeter (1924), among others.[9] Below are some important reasons Mark is regarded as the first written gospel.

1. Patterns of Order and Agreement Among the Synoptic Gospels

When we compare the Synoptic Gospels with one another, we find a tremendous amount of verbatim agreement, but what is even more striking is that both Matthew and Luke appear to follow Mark's sequencing of events consistently. There are instances in which Matthew departs from the sequence we find in Mark, and the same is true for Luke. However, there are no instances in which both Matthew and Luke together depart from Mark's ordering of material. From this angle, it seems a strong likelihood that Matthew and Luke both employed Mark's essential framework when developing their narratives and departed from it only when each wanted to share a particular story or emphasize an event.

2. The Quality of Mark's Greek and Writing Style

Mark's Greek is the roughest of the four Gospels and among the most elementary in the NT. The differences in style between the three Gospels can be more easily explained as Matthew and Luke correcting Mark's poor grammar, vocabulary, etc. These sorts of corrections are particularly noticeable when we compare Mark's limited use of Greek

---

9. Important works include: Karl Lachmann, "De ordine narrationum in evangeliis synopticis," [An English translation of the Latin title: "On the Order of the Narratives in the Synoptic Gospels"] *Theologische Studien und Kritiken* 8 (1835): 570–90; H. J. Holtzmann, *Die synoptischen Evangelien ihr Ursprung und geschichtlicher Charakter* [*The Origin and Historical Character of the Synoptic Gospels*] (Leipzig: Verlag von Wilhelm Engelmann, 1863); F. C. Burkitt, *The Gospel History and Its Transmission* (Edinburgh: T&T Clark, 1906), and B. H. Streeter, *The Four Gospels: A Study of Origins, Treating of the Manuscript Tradition, Sources, Authorship, and Dates* (London: Macmillan, 1924).

prepositions to the broader and more variegated use of prepositions by Matthew and Luke. Additionally, scholars have noted that Mark's text has numerous literary redundancies, and these were sometimes explained in the past as Markan conflations of Matthew and Luke. However, the evidence is better accounted for if we see Matthew and Luke removing these redundancies by choosing one of Mark's constructions and omitting the other. For Matthew and Luke, this choice has the net effect of smoothing out their respective texts.

3. Amount of Shared Material

Altogether, Mark has 678 verses, 601 of which are found between both Matthew and Luke. Roughly 90 percent of Mark's material appears in Matthew and over 60 percent appears in Luke. Only four of Mark's 88 pericopes are missing from Matthew and Luke. Understanding the data in this way more easily accounts for the existence of shared material across the three Gospels.

For these reasons and others, Markan priority has become the standard view among NT scholars today.[10] This realization has caused modern gospel researchers to rethink a great deal about the historical reception of the fourfold gospel, especially Mark's reception within the early church. It also had the unintended (but necessary) effect of placing Mark at the center of some of the most important deliberations among scholars working on the earliest gospel traditions. As a consequence, more material has been written on the Gospel of Mark in the past two centuries than in the previous 1,800 years.

---

10. For a helpful and detailed treatment of Markan priority, see Mark Goodacre, *The Synoptic Problem: A Way Through the Maze*, Understanding the Bible and Its World (London: Continuum, 2004), 56–83.

Source Criticism and Form Criticism: Mark as Arranger/ Compiler

The identification of Mark as the earliest written gospel had implications for questions about gospel interrelations. If Mark was written first, the next obvious questions concern how the other evangelists made use of Mark. It became clear to researchers that the high level of verbatim agreement among the synoptic evangelists was not due to the inspiration of the Holy Spirit—as had long been asserted—but to the creative use and incorporation of multiple written traditions.[11] The quest to solve the puzzle of the *written sources* behind our gospel traditions is known as "source criticism."

Modern gospel studies were born out of the work of the source critics. Their primary goal was to wrestle with the interrelationships between our canonical texts and to propose solutions to the Synoptic problem. This fruitful area of research remains foundational to what we do in gospel research today. That said, other important developments were necessary to propel us forward in our understanding of the composition, transmission, and reception of the Gospels. A clear strength of source criticism's overall agenda was its sober emphasis on the final texts as a compilation of other written sources. It is critical for us to realize that these texts did not emerge from one person sitting and composing a document from start to finish. Rather, whoever was responsible for the final version of Mark made use of multiple sources, written and oral—even if, in some cases, we no longer have access to those sources. In addition, the other synoptic evangelists used

---

11. Among those who saw the verbatim agreement as simply a byproduct of divine inspiration, an important realization was that, in numerous places, the Gospels also recorded things that were conflicting or even irreconcilable. Should these also be attributed to the inspiration of the Holy Spirit?

Mark as their primary source text along with other material to which we no longer have direct access.

One weakness of source criticism, however, was an underdeveloped understanding of the text as a mere "compilation" and the final author/editor as an unsophisticated "compiler." This idea persisted in the work of the form critics, who built on the work of the source critics while raising a new set of questions to consider. As we trace here the movement from source and form criticisms, through redaction criticism and into narrative and rhetorical approaches, we will see that each successive methodology retained the best insights of those that preceded it while abandoning those ideas or assumptions that were no longer considered valuable. The notion of the evangelists as artless compilers is one of those ideas that needed to be abandoned, as we will see below.

Form criticism emerged partially in response to some of the perceived weaknesses in the approach of source critics. The form critics saw the Synoptic Gospels not as literature in the classical sense but as a form of "folk literature" that developed over time and in community. This methodology emerged partially from an awareness of the high levels of illiteracy in Roman Palestine and its environs in the first century CE. Earliest Christian communities likely communicated important elements of the Jesus tradition through oral transmission. According to the form critics, this oral communication took the form of various units or folk literary "forms" that circulated as independent units. Thus, form criticism sought to classify these independent units and trace them back to the period of transmission within the early church. Like the construction of a knock-knock joke in our contemporary world, these "forms" were structured in a fixed way and could easily be committed to memory. Examples of these forms as envisioned by the form critics include parables, miracle stories, tales, legends, and aphorisms, among others.[12] Along with identifying these units, the form critics also sought to determine each unit's historical context within the broader literary tradition, and this led to an emphasis on the "life setting" (*Sitz im Leben*) of the community that generated these forms. This emphasis had the unintended consequence of taking the focus of study away from the text itself and focusing more on the life of the community that generated and preserved these forms. While recognizing that this literature, like all classic literature, was functioning at two levels—the world behind the text and the world within the text—the form critics placed most of their emphasis on the former to the neglect of the latter. This resulted in a focus on reconstructing the world behind the text and very often defending the veracity of these reconstructions with great conviction, while virtually ignoring the world of the text.

The form critics also doubled down on the source critical claim that the evangelists were artless compilers rather than creative authors/editors. This is perhaps most clearly seen in Martin Dibelius's well-known assertion: "The literary understanding of the synoptics begins with the recognition that they are *collections of material*. The composers are only to the smallest extent authors. *They are principally collectors, vehicles of tradition, editors*."[13] In the writings of many form critics one can also detect a historically provincial tone that judges the accomplishments of the Gospel writers as lacking in sophistication. Despite the positive contributions of the form critics, their understanding of the role of the Gospel writer as collector/complier was in need of further nuance.

---

12. These forms are spelled out in greater detail in Edgar V. McKnight, *What Is Form Criticism?* GBS (Minneapolis: Fortress, 1969).

13. Martin Dibelius, *From Tradition to Gospel*, trans. B. L. Woolf (Cambridge: James Clarke, 1971), 3 (emphasis added). The original German appeared as *Die Formsgeschichte des Evangeliums* (Tübingen: Mohr Siebeck, 1919).

At the end of the day, source critics and form critics alike were concerned with the use and arrangement of sources. Source critics were primarily interested in the employment of *written sources* while the form critics were focused on the incorporation of various *orally derived and orally transmitted sources* (i.e., "forms"). At the heart of their considerations was an embrace of Markan priority, which by that time had become a canon of critical orthodoxy. Long neglected in the formation of early Christian doctrines, the Second Gospel found a second life as it lay at the heart of those conversations within source and form criticisms.

Redaction Criticism: Mark as Theologian

Redaction criticism emerged in the 1950s and concerned itself with the ways various sources had been collected, arranged, and edited to establish each evangelist's unique theological perspective. This new approach built on the most important insights of source and form criticisms; it arose out of the conviction that, while the Gospels were made up of written and orally derived sources, each also had a *specific theological perspective*. Thus, the Gospel writers were more than simply compilers of tradition; they were sophisticated theologians in their own right. This critical insight can be seen in the very title of Willi Marxsen's foundational work, *Mark the Evangelist*—the earliest monograph applying redaction criticism to one of the Gospels.[14] To describe Mark as an

---

14. Willi Marxsen, *Mark the Evangelist: Studies on the Redaction History of the Gospel*, trans. James Boyce (Nashville: Abingdon, 1979). The original German appeared as *Der Evangelist Markus: Studien zur Redaktionsgeschichte des Evangeliums*, FRLANT 49 (Göttingen: Vandenhoeck & Ruprecht, 1956). Following this publication on Mark, two foundational works appeared, one devoted to Luke and the other to Matthew. See Hans Conzelmann, *The Theology of St. Luke*, trans. Geoffrey Buswell (New York: Harper & Row, 1961), and Günther Bornkamm, Gerhard Barth, and Heinz Joachim Held, *Tradition and Interpretation in Matthew* (Philadelphia: Westminster, 1963).

"evangelist" meant that he exercised theological creativity in the formation of the final document, an important idea in light of the source and form critical rejection of the creative role of the Gospel writers.

Like the form critics before them, redaction critics were also concerned with the life setting (*Sitz im Leben*) of the evangelists and devoted significant attention to uncovering the circumstances of the communities in which the Gospels emerged. This emphasis led to an ironic scenario: redaction criticism began with the assertion that those responsible for piecing together the texts in their final forms had a specific theological agenda and that the written Gospel was the vehicle for the unfolding of that agenda. However, a major problem in the execution of this methodology was that its practitioners rarely, if ever, read the Gospel texts from start to finish in a way that would help to show *how the evangelists had generated unique theological portraits of Jesus.* Instead, they were more often concerned with tracing untidy literary seams, proposing theories of rearrangement within the text, and speculating about the life of the Markan, Matthean, or Lukan communities.

The redaction critics accepted Markan priority and the source critical emphasis on the presence of shared written sources in the Synoptic Gospels. They also accepted the form critical emphasis on the presence of orally derived and orally transmitted sources. However, they jettisoned the idea that the authors of the Gospels were collectors/compilers in favor of a more nuanced understanding of the authors as evangelists/theologians. They placed a pronounced emphasis on the world behind the text but often failed to trace the unfolding theological rhetoric of the text. All of this led to a question: If the Gospels are, in fact, creative theological treatises, who will read these texts with a view to uncovering the distinctive theological rhetoric of each evangelist? Enter the narrative critics.

Narrative, Literary, and Rhetorical Criticisms: Mark as Storyteller

By the late 1970s redaction criticism was the dominant interpretive framework within which gospel scholars were working. Much of the discussion in gospel studies was focused on reconstructing the world behind the text but very little attention was given to what might be called a "close reading" of the text from start to finish. A restlessness began to emerge among some who had been employing redaction critical methods but also wanted to read the text on its own terms. It also seemed clear to some that a large segment of redaction-critical scholarship offered few measurable results. This frustration led to the employment of a new method that drew largely from the so-called "New Criticism" being employed in the study of English literature. The Gospel of Mark was again at the center of these developments.

In 1979, Robert Tannehill published his foundational article, "The Gospel of Mark as Narrative Christology," in which he systematically examined the elements of Mark's story world with the goal of uncovering Mark's distinctive literary and theological rhetoric.[15] This article was one of a handful of publications that ushered in a new approach known as narrative criticism. Building on the best ideas of source, form, and redaction criticisms, the narrative critics introduced a new insight: the Gospel writers were not just evangelists/theologians but were also sophisticated

---

15. Robert C. Tannehill, "The Gospel of Mark as Narrative Christology," *Semeia* 16 (1979): 57–95.

storytellers.[16] Thus, if we are to reckon with the theological rhetoric of the text, we must employ the methods of literary criticism to the text as it exists in its final form (i.e., a close reading of literary elements within the text itself).

In 1982, David Rhoads—one of the pioneers of narrative criticism—published his article "Narrative Criticism and the Gospel of Mark,"[17] and shortly after this, Rhoads's collaboration with Shakespearean scholar Donald Michie was published as *Mark as Story*[18]—the first book to apply narrative criticism to one of the four Gospels.[19] In the years immediately following this important publication, scholars would devote individual treatises to all four canonical Gospels and Acts, before branching off into more parochial narrative concerns.[20] Between the

---

16. While I will not cover the subject matter here, recent years have seen an emphasis on Mark within ancient oral and performance contexts. While these authors make the case that such an approach can stand on its own, there is little doubt that performative approaches arose out of a narrative-critical framework and its understanding of Mark as a storyteller. For more on the interface between narrative and performance-oriented approaches, see Kelly R. Iverson, ed., *From Text to Performance: Narrative and Performance Criticisms in Dialogue and Debate*, Biblical Performance Criticism (Eugene, OR: Cascade, 2014); and Zechariah P. Eberhart and Christopher W. Skinner, eds., "Narrative and Performance Criticisms—A Difference of Degree or Kind?," *Religions* 14.8/9 (2023).

17. David Rhoads, "Narrative Criticism and the Gospel of Mark," *JAAR* 50.3 (1982): 411–34.

18. David Rhoads and Donald Michie, *Mark as Story: An Introduction to the Narrative of a Gospel* (Minneapolis: Fortress, 1982). This book is now in a third edition (2012). Joanna Dewey, another pioneer in narrative criticism, served as co-author on the second (1999) and third editions.

19. For a more fulsome history of the early impact of narrative criticism, see Christopher W. Skinner, "Telling the Story: The Appearance and Impact of *Mark as Story*," in *Mark as Story: Retrospect and Prospect*, ed. Kelly R. Iverson and Christopher W. Skinner, RBS (Atlanta: Society of Biblical Literature, 2012).

20. Some important early works include: R. Alan Culpepper, *Anatomy of the Fourth Gospel: A Study in Literary Design* (Minneapolis: Fortress, 1983); Robert C. Tannehill, *The Narrative Unity of Luke-Acts: A Literary Interpretation*, 2 vols. (Minneapolis: Fortress, 1986–89); Jack Dean Kingsbury, *Matthew as Story* (Minneapolis: Augsburg Fortress, 1988); Kingsbury, *Conflict in Mark: Jesus, Authorities, Disciples* (Minneapolis: Fortress, 1989); Mark Allan Powell, *What Is Narrative Criticism?* GBS (Minneapolis: Fortress, 1990); Robert M. Fowler, *Let the Reader Understand: Reader-Response Criticism and the Gospel of Mark* (Minneapolis: Fortress, 1991).

early 1980s and the 2000s, narrative criticism continued to evolve and exert its influence in various quarters of gospel studies. Today this method is regularly employed by those working with the NT narratives.

Narrative criticism accepts that the Gospels are made up of written sources (source criticism) and orally derived sources (form criticism), while also accepting that each evangelist had a theological perspective to share (redaction criticism). However, while these methods took a more piecemeal approach to the texts, narrative critics wanted to consider these texts in their final forms, irrespective of the various stages and phases of their composition. This meant paying attention to the rhetoric of the text: the development of plot, the role of characters and characterization, and the deployment of themes and motifs, among other things.

In the thematic chapters that follow, this is the approach I will employ. I approach the Gospel with an acceptance of the important contributions of source, form, and redaction criticisms while also focusing on the world within the text. I will raise historical questions throughout, but my coverage of each theme will also attempt to show how Mark's uniquely crafted story provides us with his own distinctive theological contribution to the canon of Scripture.

THE GOSPEL OF MARK AND CHRISTIAN THEOLOGY IN PROSPECT

The foregoing discussion represents an abbreviated history of important methodological shifts over the past two-and-a-half centuries. Looking back, we can confidently assert that the Gospel of Mark had a relatively insignificant impact on the shape of early Christian teaching on theology and ethics. Though it was virtually ignored for centuries, Mark eventually emerged as a text of critical importance to our modern understanding of the written gospel tradition. But this is not all. The Gospel of Mark continues to spawn new areas of interest in the study of earliest Christianity. Mark's Gospel is currently situated at the center of studies on ancient orality and performance,[21] cognitive narratology,[22] early Christian book culture,[23] social memory,[24] ritual studies,[25] and characterization,[26] among others. Mark's importance may have been overlooked by the early church, but its contemporary pride of position appears fixed.

---

21. Whitney Shiner, *Proclaiming the Gospel: First-Century Performance of Mark* (Harrisburg, PA: Trinity Press International, 2003); Kelly R. Iverson, *Performing Early Christian Literature: Audience Experience and Interpretation of the Gospels* (Cambridge, UK: Cambridge University Press, 2021); and Zechariah P. Eberhart, *Between Script and Scripture: Performance Criticism and Mark's Characterization of the Disciples*, BibInt 220 (Leiden: Brill, 2024).

22. Jan Rüggemeier, "Mark's Narrative Christology following the Cognitive Turn. Developments, Implications, and Desiderata of an Interpretative Concept and Its Impact on the Analysis of Mark 1:21–28," *EC* 12.3 (2021): 322–45; Kirsten Marie Hartvigsen, *Prepare the Way of the Lord: Towards a Cognitive Poetic Analysis of Audience Involvement with Characters and Events in the Markan World*, BZNW 180 (Berlin: deGruyter, 2012).

23. Matthew D. C. Larsen, *Gospels Before the Book* (Oxford: Oxford University Press, 2018); Chris Keith, *The Gospel as Manuscript: An Early History of the Jesus Tradition as Material Artifact* (Oxford: Oxford University Press, 2020).

24. Sandra Huebenthal, *Reading Mark's Gospel as a Text from Collective Memory* (Grand Rapids: Eerdmans, 2020).

25. Paul D. Wheatley, "The Ritual Bridge Between Narrative and Performance in the Gospel of Mark," *Religions* 14.9 (2023): 1104; https://doi.org/10.3390/rel14091104; Wheatley, "Mark as Ritual Narrative: Anointing, Memorial, and Genre Signifiers in Mark 14:3–9," *CBQ* 85.3 (2023): 465–84.

26. Christopher W. Skinner and Matthew Ryan Hauge, eds., *Character Studies and the Gospel of Mark*, LNTS 483 (London: Bloomsbury/T&T Clark, 2014); Michael R. Whitenton, *Hearing Kyriotic Sonship: A Cognitive and Rhetorical Approach to the Characterization of Mark's Jesus*, BibInt 148 (Leiden: Brill, 2016).

FIGURE 2.1: CRITICAL METHODOLOGIES IN GOSPEL RESEARCH
(1780s TO 2020s)

	Source Criticism	**Form Criticism**
Approach	Identify the written sources behind the final form of our extant texts.	Identify and classify the different forms of oral tradition in our extant texts. Also explain how they functioned in the so-called "life setting" (*Sitz im Leben*) of the early Christian communities.
View of the Author	The evangelist is not an author but a collector and complier of written sources.	The evangelist is not an author but a collector and compiler of units that circulated in oral tradition.[*]
Time Period Under Consideration	The time of composition.	The era prior to formal composition when materials were still circulating and being transmitted orally.
View of the Final Product	A compilation of written sources.	A "folk" document consisting of both written and orally derived sources.

*Form critics did not deny the presence of written sources but primarily emphasized orally transmitted sources, or "forms."

Redaction Criticism	Narrative Criticism
Identify the motivations for and methods behind the editorial decisions of the editor (redactor). Also discern as much as possible about the life setting (*Sitz im Leben*) of the text.	Read the narrative as an autonomous composition on its own terms and without appeal to the other Gospel portraits.
The evangelist is a sophisticated theologian who has edited the composition with a specific theological focus and end in mind.	The evangelist is both a theologian and a storyteller who has crafted the composition with specific theological foci and intends a specific rhetorical effect on the audience.
The *Sitz im Leben* of the author and/or community to whom the author is writing.	The narrative time as it is consequential to the overall literary presentation.
A theological treatise.	An autonomous narrative.

FOR FURTHER READING

A. Source, Form, and Redaction Criticisms, Markan Priority, and the Synoptic Problem

Bultmann, Rudolf K., *The History of the Synoptic Tradition.*
    Translated by John Marsh. New York: Harper & Row, 1963.

Burkitt, F. C. *The Gospel History and Its Transmission.* Edinburgh:
    T&T Clark, 1906.

Goodacre, Mark. *The Synoptic Problem: A Way Through the Maze.* Under-
    standing the Bible and Its World. London: Continuum, 2004.

Marxsen, Willi. *Mark the Evangelist: Studies on the Redaction History
    of the Gospel.* Translated by James Boyce. Nashville: Abingdon,
    1969.

McKnight, Edgar V. *What Is Form Criticism?* GBS. Minneapolis:
    Fortress, 1969.

Perrin, Norman. *What Is Redaction Criticism?* GBS. Minneapolis:
    Fortress, 1969.

Porter, Stanley E., and Bryan Dyer, eds. *The Synoptic Problem: Four
    Views.* Grand Rapids: Baker Academic, 2016.

Streeter, B. H. *The Four Gospels: A Study of Origins, Treating of the
    Manuscript Tradition, Sources, Authorship, and Dates.* London:
    Macmillan, 1924.

B. Narrative, Literary, and Rhetorical Readings of Mark

Dewey, Joanna, David Rhoads, and Donald Michie, *Mark as Story:
    An Introduction to the Narrative of a Gospel.* 3rd ed. Minneapolis:
    Fortress, 2012.

Fowler, Robert M. *Let the Reader Understand: Reader-Response Criticism
    and the Gospel of Mark.* Minneapolis: Fortress, 1991.

Iverson, Kelly R. *Reading Mark*, Cascade Companions. Eugene, OR:
    Cascade, 2023.

Juel, Donald. *A Master of Surprise: Mark Interpreted.* Minneapolis:
    Fortress, 2002.

Kingsbury, Jack Dean. *Conflict in Mark: Jesus, Authorities, Disciples.*
    Minneapolis: Fortress, 1989.

Moloney, Francis J. *Mark: Storyteller, Interpreter, Evangelist.* Peabody,
    MA: Hendrickson, 2004.

Powell, Mark Allan. "Narrative Criticism: The Emergence of a Prominent Reading Strategy." In *Mark as Story: Retrospect and Prospect*, edited by Kelly R. Iverson and Christopher W. Skinner, 19–43. RBS 65. Atlanta: Society of Biblical Literature, 2011.

Stock, Augustine. *Call to Discipleship: A Literary Study of Mark's Gospel*, Good News Studies 1. Wilmington, DE: Michael Glazier, 1982.

C. Characterization, Cognitive Narratology, Early Christian Book Culture, Orality, Performance

Eberhart, Zechariah P. *Between Script and Scripture: A Proposal for Biblical Performance Criticism*. BibInt 220. Leiden: Brill, 2024.

Iverson, Kelly R. *Performing Early Christian Literature: Audience Experience and Interpretation of the Gospels*. Cambridge, UK: Cambridge University Press, 2021.

Keith, Chris. *The Gospel as Manuscript: An Early History of the Jesus Tradition as Material Artifact*. Oxford: Oxford University Press, 2020.

Larsen, Matthew D. C. *Gospels Before the Book*. Oxford: Oxford University Press, 2018.

Rhoads, David. "Performance Criticism: An Emerging Methodology in Second Testament Studies—Part I." *BTB* 36.3 (2006): 1–16.

Rhoads, David. "Performance Criticism: An Emerging Methodology in Second Testament Studies—Part II," *BTB* 36.4 (2006): 164–84.

Rüggemeier, Jan, and Elizabeth Shively, eds., "Cognitive Linguistics and New Testament Narrative: Investigating Methodology through Characterization." Special issue of *BibInt* 29.4–5 (2021).

Shiner, Whitney. *Proclaiming the Gospel: First-Century Performance of Mark*. Harrisburg, PA: Trinity Press International, 2003.

Skinner, Christopher W., and Matthew Ryan Hauge, eds., *Character Studies and the Gospel of Mark*. LNTS 483. London: Bloomsbury/T&T Clark, 2014.

Whitenton, Michael R. *Hearing Kyriotic Sonship: A Cognitive and Rhetorical Approach to the Characterization of Mark's Jesus*. BibInt 148. Leiden: Brill, 2016.

CHAPTER 3

"Who Is This Man?" (Part 1)

Jesus the Messiah

The first theme we will consider here is Mark's emphasis on the identity of Jesus. The Gospel of Mark is first
and foremost a narrative about Jesus Christ, the Son of God.
Therefore, it makes sense to begin our discussion of Markan
themes with a focus on the specific contours of Mark's presentation of Jesus. The identity of Jesus is the overarching
theme that guides Mark's narrative and, as we will see below,
punctuates the critical moments in the story.

In the late 1970s, Robert Tannehill referred to the Gospel
of Mark as a "narrative Christology." In coining this terminology, he stated that his aim was, in part, to take "seriously
the narrative form of Mark in discussing this Gospel's presentation of Jesus Christ."[1] In my approach to Mark in this
book as a narrative Christology, I begin by recognizing the
all-pervasive question that appears in various forms throughout the narrative: "Who is this man?" Sometimes the question

---

1. See Robert C. Tannehill, "The Gospel of Mark as Narrative Christology,"
Semeia 16 (1979): 57–95. One of the more important works on Mark's Christology
in recent years takes its cue from Tannehill's original description while expand-
ing on it in significant ways. See Elizabeth Struthers Malbon, *Mark's Jesus:
Characterization as Narrative Christology* (Waco, TX: Baylor University Press, 2009).

of Jesus's identity is answered before it can even be raised (1:11, 24, 34; 3:11; 5:6), and sometimes it is the subject of wider conversation and speculation (3:22–30; 6:2–3, 14–16). At other times, the question appears in moments of genuine awe and bewilderment (1:27; 4:41). On one occasion, Jesus himself poses the question to his disciples (8:27–31). This question certainly drives Mark's narrative and is particularly prominent in the first half of the Gospel (1:1–8:31). While some figures in the story struggle to come to terms with Jesus's identity, Mark has ensured that the reader will be able to answer this question with some degree of clarity. He begins with the fundamental declaration that Jesus is the Christ and Son of God (1:1).[2] These two titles provide us with the primary framework for understanding Mark's Christology throughout the narrative. While "Christ" and "Son of God" are not all that Mark affirms about Jesus, they set the principal parameters for his distinctive portrait.[3] As Jack Dean Kingsbury noted over forty years ago, "since Mark has told the reader in 1:1 that Jesus is the Messiah, the Son of God, the reader can rest assured that this understanding of Jesus will have the sanction of God in Mark's story and

---

2. It is important to acknowledge a major text-critical issue here, with disagreement among scholars over whether the phrase "son of God" (Greek: *huiou theou*) is original to the text of 1:1. See the thorough treatment of the evidence and an argument for the omission of "son of God," in Adela Yarbro Collins, *Mark*, Hermeneia (Minneapolis: Fortress, 2007), 130–32. For a clear presentation that favors the longer reading, see Tommy Wasserman, "The 'Son of God' Was in the Beginning (Mark 1:1)," *JTS* 62.1 (2011): 20–50. There is not space in this chapter to make a full argument for my position, though I am persuaded that the longer reading "Jesus Christ, the Son of God" is to be preferred for numerous reasons. This textual decision is critical to my understanding of Mark's Christology and will inform the next two chapters and much of the book.

3. Other titles ascribed to Jesus in Mark include, the Holy One of God (1:24), Teacher (4:38; 9:17, 38; 10:17, 20, 35; 12:14, 19, 32; 13:1), Rabbi (11:21; 14:45), Son of David (10:47; 12:35), and prophet (6:4; 8:28).

hence be the 'normative understanding.'"[4] However, even if this description represents the normative understanding of Jesus from the evaluative point of view of Mark's narrator— and I agree that it does—what does it actually mean *for Mark* to affirm that Jesus is both Christ and Son of God?[5]

At least two potential complications arise when trying to answer this question. First, over the centuries, both titles have evolved in what they signify, and both represent different things to different groups of Christian readers. This means that a certain level of "unlearning" is required for well-meaning readers of the Bible to think about these titles in their ancient rather than their contemporary contexts. Second, and perhaps more problematically, scholars vary in their opinions about what these titles originally signified and how they function within Mark against the backdrop of his social and religious contexts, including Hellenistic Judaism and the realities of Roman occupation. Thus, a lengthier discussion of these two titles and how they are used in Mark is needed. We will pursue these questions over the next two chapters. The present chapter focuses on the background of Messiah concepts and how we ought to understand Jesus as the Messiah in the Gospel of Mark. The next chapter is devoted to understanding the Son of God formulation against

---

4. Jack Dean Kingsbury, *The Christology of Mark's Gospel* (Philadelphia: Fortress, 1983), 57.

5. Throughout this chapter I will use "Messiah" and "Christ" interchangeably, as the terms are synonymous—one arising from Hebrew/Aramaic and the other from Greek and both meaning "anointed one." In Hebrew/Aramaic, the term Messiah (Hebrew: *mashiach*; Aramaic *maschiacha*) is the participial form of the verb *mashach*, "to anoint." In Greek, the term Christ (Greek: *christos*) is the participial form of the verb *chriō*, "to anoint." While there is significant debate among scholars as to whether some writers—most notably Paul—understand *christos* as simply a name or as a title, it is clear that Mark is using *christos* as a title throughout his Gospel.

its Jewish and Roman backgrounds to better understand how Mark presents Jesus as the Son of God. Once we have established the understanding of Christ and Son of God that will guide our discussions throughout this book, we will be in a better position to answer the question that drives Mark's narrative: "Who is this man?"

MESSIANIC CONCEPTS IN THE FIRST CENTURY CE

Each semester I ask students about their understanding of the word "Messiah." I invariably get numerous responses, most of which carry the weight of centuries of Christian theological development but have little to do with the concepts of Messiah that arise within the Bible. For example, students will identify a messiah as one who suffers for good or as one who provides "salvation" in some spiritual sense. Others will opine that someone with a "messiah complex" feels as though they need to "save the world." Still others will draw a connection between the concept of messiah and a martyr's death. One of the more pervasive ideas that arises is that a messiah figure is supposed to be divine. These ideas no doubt derive from broader cultural usage and also likely from teaching to which my students have been exposed in some Christian context, but they are ultimately foreign to the Judaisms of the first century CE. Mark is doing something distinctive in the way he presents Jesus as Messiah. However, his literary and theological agendas can be difficult to discern in a world that has conflated the meaning of Messiah with so many other foreign and often later understandings of the term. To appreciate how Mark deploys the language of Messiah in reference to Jesus, we need first to trace the concept historically as it evolved within the Jewish world.[6] Only then will we be able to understand Mark's use of Messiah in its literary context.

What Is an "Anointed One"?

When many Christian readers of the NT think of the term Messiah or Anointed One, their understanding often includes nuances related to royal, prophetic, or priestly functions. Some of this can be traced back to the Protestant Reformation and John Calvin's well-known formulation of Jesus as "prophet, king, and priest."[7] As mentioned in the previous chapter, readers commonly impose their highly developed theological ideas onto our ancient text without considering how this might be an illegitimate approach. Other Christian readers of the NT subscribe to interpretive traditions that find in Jesus specific prophetic fulfillments of Hebrew Bible passages, which they assume have highly developed messianic expectations. This is, in fact, how some of the NT writers—particularly Matthew and Luke—present Jesus's messianic status, so we should not be surprised that some faith communities also understand Jesus in this way. This latter phenomenon places a great deal of emphasis on the presence of so-called messianic prophecies in the Hebrew Bible.

Despite occasional claims to the contrary, there is no unified understanding of a coming messianic figure in the

---

6. In his insightful book, *The Grammar of Messianism: An Ancient Jewish Political Idiom and Its Users* (Oxford: Oxford University Press, 2017), Matthew Novenson makes the critical point that everyone who deploys the language of Messiah during this period is doing something distinctive. It is therefore disingenuous to suggest that there is a standard understanding of Messiah during the Second Temple period, even if there are some common elements within the texts that speak of such a figure.

7. "In order that faith may find a firm basis for salvation in Christ, and thus rest in him, this principle must be laid down: the office enjoined upon Christ by the Father consists of three parts. For he was given to be *prophet, king, and priest*" (John Calvin, *Institutes of the Christian Religion*, 2 vols., ed. John T. McNeill [Louisville: Westminster John Knox, 1960], 1.494 [emphasis added]).

Hebrew Bible, Second Temple Judaism, or even in early Christianity. By the first century CE, numerous messianic expectations were reflected to varying degrees in different Jewish texts, but none of them share a one-to-one correspondence with depictions of those described as "God's anointed" in the Hebrew Bible or in the various presentations of Jesus in the NT. The more evolved messianic ideas we see at work in the NT and in early Christianity emerged in the Second Temple period, though they will make little sense to us without some understanding of how the concept first emerged in the Hebrew Bible.

The term "anointed one" (Hebrew: *maschiach*), which arose from the Hebrew Bible, did not begin its life as a static concept. Appearing thirty-nine times, *maschiach* is most regularly used of kings (e.g., 1 Sam 12:3, 5; 24:6; 2 Sam 1:14; 19:21), though it is also used of priests (e.g., Lev 4:3, 5, 16; 6:22) and patriarchs (1 Chr 16:22; Ps 105:15).[8] In ancient Israel, both people and objects were smeared (i.e., "anointed") with oil in ritual contexts as a way of bestowing sacredness. This was a well-attested practice throughout the ancient Near East. Thus, the use of the term "anointed one," particularly in its application to Israel's leaders, denotes being sanctioned by God for a specific purpose. Its use likely assumes that the audience had some familiarity with the installation of kings that included a ritual anointing with oil, even after that practice was abandoned. However, when the biblical writers

---

8. The term never occurs in the Hebrew Bible with only the definite article and the noun (i.e., "the Messiah"; Hebrew: *ha maschiach*). Rather, some sort of modifier is regularly in place between the two (e.g., "my anointed one," "the Lord's anointed one," "his anointed one," etc.). The term appears twice without an article or modifier. For a full list of occurrences, see Lev 4:3, 5, 16; 6:22; 1 Sam 2:10, 35; 12:3, 5; 16:6; 24:6 (twice), 10; 26:9, 11, 16, 23; 2 Sam 1:14, 16, 21; 19:21; 22:51; 23:1; 1 Chr 16:22; 2 Chr 6:42; Pss 2:2; 18:50; 20:6; 28:8; 84:9; 89:38, 51; 105:15; 132:10, 17; Isa 45:1; Lam 4:20; Dan 9:25, 26; Hab 3:13.

applied the term "anointed one" to these various figures, they did not have in mind the full constellation of royal, eschatological, and priestly ideas so often associated with Messiah in early Christian texts and in later rabbinic Judaism, nor did they have in mind contemporary Christian theological doctrines.[9]

To understand the appearance of this term throughout the NT, and particularly its use in the Gospel of Mark, we must turn to some of the other sacred Jewish writings from the Second Temple period for a clearer frame of reference. Here we will briefly survey examples from three different literary corpora and show how each shares common features with the others while also betraying different understandings of what a messianic figure was expected to be and/or accomplish. We ought to note that the vision of Messiah that arises here is not singular, nor does it develop in a linear way across the various texts we will examine. We must also point out that we are only looking at texts that explicitly use the term Messiah. Numerous other texts in the Second Temple Jewish literature speak of and describe a messianic figure without using the specific term *maschiach*.[10] We do not have space to consider those in this chapter, though they also contribute to the broader discussion of messianic ideas that developed outside the Hebrew Bible leading up to the time of Jesus.

---

9. Within the NT and among later rabbinic authors, the Messiah is a royal figure who will play an important role in the last days as God's agent on earth. Contemporary Christian theologies have capitalized on this idea in their formulations of Messiah.

10. Two important examples are found in the *Testament of Levi* 18 and the *Testament of Judah* 24, both of which are in the second century BCE work *Testaments of the Twelve Patriarchs*. Both describe a coming messianic figure. For comparative purposes, the late first-century works 4 Ezra and 2 Baruch are also significant as they envision the advent of a messianic figure with many similarities to presentations of Jesus in the NT.

*Messianic Passages Outside the Hebrew Bible (Third
Century BCE–First Century CE)*

Psalms of Solomon 17 and 18 (First Century BCE)

The group of eighteen hymns, laments, and songs of
wisdom known as the Psalms of Solomon (Pss. Sol.) were
likely written in Hebrew in the first century BCE, though
only Greek and Syriac translations survive today. The psalms
are not currently accepted in the Protestant, Catholic, or
Orthodox biblical canons, though scholars often point to the
psalms for a more immediately relevant background to some
of the messianic ideas present in the NT. Written against
the backdrop of the Roman general Pompey's conquest of
Jerusalem in 63 BCE, the Psalms of Solomon reflect a range
of concerns, including an interest in Jewish cultic rituals
and a belief in resurrection. The collection begins with a
lament for the sinful children of Jerusalem (Pss. Sol. 1) and
culminates with the anticipation of a royal Messiah (Pss. Sol.
17, 18).

In Pss. Sol. 17, the psalmist writes in anticipation of the
messianic king's arrival. Robert Wright refers to this psalm as
"an extended messianic hymn describing the anticipated victory and reign of the expected redeeming king, the anointed
Son of David."[11] He will lead the faithful against their enemies and "establish an independent and holy theocratic state
to which foreign inhabitants would be subordinate."[12] Verses
20–21 contrast a wicked ruler with a coming king, the "Son
of David," that God will soon raise up. In verses 30–32, the
psalm continues:

---

11. Robert B. Wright, ed., *The Psalms of Solomon: A Critical Addition of the Greek
Text,* Jewish and Christian Texts in Context and Related Studies 1 (London: T&T
Clark, 2007), 1.

12. Wright, *Psalms of Solomon,* 1.

And he shall have the peoples of the nations to be subject
to him under his yoke. And he shall glorify the Lord in
the mark of all the earth. And he shall purify Ierousalem
[Jerusalem] in holiness as it was in the beginning so that
nations may come from the end of the earth to see his
glory, bringing as gifts her sons who are exhausted and
to see the glory of the Lord with which God has glorified
her. And he shall be a righteous king, taught by God, over
them, and there shall be no injustice in his days in their
midst, for he shall be holy, and their king, *the anointed*
[Greek: *christos*] of the Lord. (Pss. Sol. 17:30–32 [emphasis
added])[13]

Kenneth Atkinson notes that this is the "most detailed pre-
Christian description of the Davidic messiah," which has
drawn "considerable scholarly interest because of its portrayal
of the Davidic messiah as *a militant 'son of David.'*"[14] This text
is of immense importance for our study of Messiah texts outside the Hebrew Bible because it is the first reference to a messianic Son of David in all extant Second Temple literature.
Later authors draw on and develop the idea of the Messiah
as a literal descendant of David who both rules as king and
wages war. Thus, the author's use of the term here is a watershed moment in the development of ancient messianic ideas.

Psalms of Solomon 18 continues the train of thought
begun in the previous psalm by including two additional references to the coming Messiah and punctuating the entire
collection with an emphasis on God's chastening rod:

---

13. Excerpts from the Psalms of Solomon are taken from the *New English
Translation of the Septuagint* (NETS), ed. Albert Pietersma and Benjamin G. Wright
(Oxford: Oxford University Press, 2007).

14. Kenneth Atkinson, *I Cried to the Lord: A Study of the Psalms of Solomon's
Historical Background and Social Setting*, JSJSup 84 (Leiden: Brill, 2004), 129
(emphasis added).

> May God cleanse Israel for the day of pity with blessing,
> for the day of election when he brings up his anointed
> one [Greek: *christou*]. Happy are those who shall live in
> those days, to see the good things of the Lord, which he
> will perform for the coming generation. Under the rod of
> discipline of the Lord's anointed [Greek: *christou*] in fear
> of his God, in wisdom of spirit and of righteousness and
> strength, to direct a man in works of righteousness in fear
> of God. (Pss. Sol. 18:5–8)

This psalm provides a final reflection that ends on an encouraging note. Atkinson writes that Pss. Sol. 1 "describes a crisis," while this final psalm in the collection "concludes with a message of hope that messiah is coming and that God controls the universe."[15]

Already in Pss. Sol. 17–18 we begin to see specific contours of the broader shape of the various visions of a forthcoming Jewish Messiah outside the Hebrew Bible. In addition to coming for the purpose of waging war against the enemies of the Lord, this Messiah will possess "biological descent from David, anointment from the Lord, and the presence of God's spirit."[16] We must keep these elements in mind as we continue to develop an understanding of the various portraits of Messiah in the Second Temple literature and in the Gospel of Mark.

1 Enoch 48 and 52 (First Century BCE–First Century CE)

One of the most important writings for understanding various Jewish ideas in the Second Temple period is 1 Enoch, a pseudonymous text ascribed to Enoch—the descendant

---

15. Atkinson, *I Cried to the Lord*, 140.
16. Atkinson, *I Cried to the Lord*, 208.

of Adam and great-grandfather of Noah.[17] This apocalyptic text clarifies the origins of demonic entities, provides
further insight into the mysterious Nephilim of Genesis 6,
and explains in greater detail the necessity of Noah's flood.
Although it was originally written in Hebrew (or possibly
Aramaic), the best complete manuscripts we currently possess are in Ethiopic and Greek. We cannot date the book with
any precision, and scholars almost universally acknowledge
that different portions of the book were written in different
periods. The portion of 1 Enoch that concerns us here is the
so-called Parables of Enoch (1 Enoch 37–71), which scholars
believe to be the latest material in the book, likely appearing
between the late first century BCE and the early first century
CE. This would place our material roughly contemporaneous
with the origins of the Jesus movement and some of our earliest Christian writings.

Throughout 1 Enoch 37–71 we find a messianic figure
who exists "even before the creation of the sun and the moon,
before the creation of the stars" (1 En. 48:6).[18] This individual is variously called the "Chosen One," "Son of Man," and
"Messiah." Since NT texts apply all three of these titles to
Jesus in some form or another, scholars have spent a great
deal of time attempting to trace the potential influence of
1 Enoch on early Christian thought. In a passage that anticipates the silencing of God's enemies, we read:

---

17. There is little doubt that 1 Enoch influences the Jewish writers of the
NT. Jude 14–15 even quotes directly from 1 En. 1:9: "It was also about these that
Enoch, in the seventh generation from Adam, prophesied, saying, 'See, the Lord
is coming with ten thousands of his holy ones, to execute judgment on all and to
convict all the ungodly of all the deeds of ungodliness that they have committed
in such an ungodly way and of all the harsh things that ungodly sinners have
spoken against him'" (NRSVue).

18. Excerpts from 1 Enoch are taken from the translation by Ephraim Isaac
in *The Old Testament Pseudepigrapha*, ed. James H. Charlesworth, vol. 1, ABRL
(New York: Doubleday, 1983), 3–89 (here 33).

On the day of their weariness, there shall be an obstacle
on the earth and they shall fall on their faces; and they
shall not rise up (again), nor anyone (be found) who will
take them with his hands and raise them up. For they have
denied the Lord of the Spirits and his Messiah [Hebrew:
mashiachō]. Blessed be the name of the Lord of Spirits!
(1 En. 48:10–11)

About this text, Nickelsburg and VanderKam have written,
"This is the first passage in the Parables that applies to the
Son of Man/Chosen One language drawn from biblical ora-
cles about the Davidic king."[19] Importantly, it is also the first
passage in this section of 1 Enoch to use the specific term
maschiach. Like a number of messianic passages in Second
Temple literature, this text alludes to Psalm 2, which begins:

> Why do the nations conspire,
>   and the peoples plot in vain?
> The kings of the earth set themselves,
>   and the rulers take counsel together,
>   against the LORD and his anointed, saying,
> "Let us burst their bonds asunder,
>   and cast their cords from us."
>
> He who sits in the heavens laughs;
>   the LORD has them in derision.
> Then he will speak to them in his wrath,
>   and terrify them in his fury, saying,
> "I have set my king on Zion, my holy hill." (Ps 2:1–6)

---

19. George W. E. Nickelsburg and James C. VanderKam, *1 Enoch 2: A Commentary on 1 Enoch Chapters 37–82*, Hermeneia (Minneapolis: Fortress, 2012), 176.

Psalm 2 appears to have been a foundational text for shaping many understandings of the Jewish Messiah during this period. Nickelsburg and VanderKam further note that "it is typical of Jewish 'messianic' theology that the figure of the latter-day king appears when rebellious and oppressive kings are the problem."[20]

A second explicit reference to Messiah is found in 1 Enoch 52:

> After those days, in the same place where I had seen all
> the secret visions, having been carried off in a wind vehicle
> and taken to the west, my eyes saw there all the secret
> things of heaven and the future things. . . . And I asked
> the angel who was going with me saying, "What are these
> things which I have seen in secret?" And he said to me, "All
> these things which you have seen happen by the authority
> of his Messiah [Hebrew: *mashiachō*] so that he may give
> orders and be praised upon the earth." (1 En. 52:1–14)

As above, this text deploys the imagery of Psalm 2, and the Messiah pictured here possesses an authority to exercise his power and the right to receive praise. Nickelsburg and VanderKam suggest that this scene is "reminiscent of Dan 7:14, where the one like a son of man is given [authority] over all nations and peoples after the destruction of the four kingdoms and their kings that have dominated the earth."[21]

As with our above analysis of the two texts from the Psalms of Solomon, we have here a messianic son of David, sent and given authority by God, anointed by God's spirit, and appearing in a military context. While these two writings

---

20. Nickelsburg and VanderKam, *1 Enoch 2*, 176.
21. Nickelsburg and VanderKam, *1 Enoch 2*, 190.

differ from one another in both provenance and focus, they share multiple, significant ideas about the coming Messiah, which suggests such views were common to different groups of Jews.

Dead Sea Scrolls (Third Century BCE–First Century CE)

Since their initial discovery at Qumran in December 1947, the enormous cache of manuscripts known as the Dead Sea Scrolls has served as a continuous source of fascination while providing a window into the life of a solitary and isolated Jewish community in the two centuries leading up to the time of Jesus. Numerous texts from Qumran show evidence of that community's variegated understandings of the Messiah. Among the ideas reflected in various Dead Sea Scrolls are the belief in a future priestly Messiah from the line of Aaron, a royal Messiah from the line of David, and a heavenly or divine Messiah. In some texts it appears that the community's enigmatic "Teacher of Righteousness," was also regarded as a messianic figure. We do not have space here to consider every messianic text from Qumran, but several are especially noteworthy and relevant to our discussion. Again, we are looking only at texts that employ the term Messiah, but it is important to remember that the Dead Sea Scrolls contain many descriptions of a messianic figure where the term *maschiach* is absent.[22]

1. Rule of the Congregation (First Century BCE)

The text known as the Rule of the Congregation (1QSa) is an appendix to one of the foundational documents discovered at Qumran—the Rule of the Community (or Manual

---

22. For a comprehensive treatment of this question, see John J. Collins, *The Scepter and the Star: The Messiahs of the Dead Sea Scrolls and Other Ancient Literature*, ABRL (New York: Doubleday, 1995).

of Discipline, 1QS). Also known as "the messianic rule," the
Rule of the Congregation contains three explicit references
to Messiah in the context of behavior during meals in the
eschatological period. He is once called "Messiah" and twice
referred to as the "Messiah of Israel":

> This is the assembly of famous men, [those summoned to]
> the gathering of the community council, when God begets
> the Messiah [Hebrew: *maschiach*] with them. . . . After [the
> Me]ssiah of Israel shall ent[er] and before him shall sit the
> chiefs [of the clans of Israel, each] one according to his
> dignity. . . . Afterwards, the Messiah of Israel shall stretch
> out his hand towards the bread. (1QSa 2:11–21)

The Messiah pictured in this document appears to be a king,
though his status is below that of the high priest—a situation
that reflects the circumstances surrounding the envisioned
reconstruction of the temple in Ezekiel 40–48. Ezekiel's
vision includes a new administration in Israel where the
greatest authority goes to the high priest, who will oversee the
temple, while the priesthood exercises primary leadership in
the restored land. Ezekiel also pictures a royal figure (a king
or perhaps a prince) who rules civic affairs while still serving
under the administration of the priesthood. This royal figure
is most likely understood as having Davidic descent, but the
Qumran community subordinates this Davidic king to the
high priest.

2. The Damascus Document (First Century BCE–First Century CE)

The text known as the Damascus Document (CD) was
already known to researchers before its discovery among
the Dead Sea Scrolls because of its inclusion in a work

published in 1910.[23] Scholars were unaware, however, of the group responsible for its composition until they also uncovered the Damascus Document at Qumran. Considered one of the foundational documents of the Essene community, the Damascus Document is hard to date with precision, though we can confidently assign a date prior to the first Jewish revolt (66–74 CE)—the event that ultimately caused the dissolution of the Essene community. The Damascus Document is unique among the texts we have examined to this point in that it appears to speak of the rise of *two messiahs*, the messiah of Aaron and messiah of Israel (something we also see in other Dead Sea Scroll texts):[24]

> Those who walk in them, in the time of wickedness until there arises the messiah [Hebrew: *mashiach*] of Aaron and Israel, they shall be ten in number as a minimum to (form) thousands, hundreds, fifties, and tens. (CD 12:23–13:2)[25]

> And this is the exact interpretation of the regulations by which [they shall be ruled] [until there arises the messiah] of Aaron and Israel. (CD 14:18–19)

---

23. Solomon Schechter, *Documents of Jewish Sectaries*, vol. 1, *Fragments of a Zadokite Work* (Cambridge, UK: Cambridge University Press, 1910). The version of the Damascus Document published by Schechter was discovered among the Cairo Genizah and is abbreviated CD.

24. While many assume that these texts constitute a reference to two figures, numerous scholars have questioned this conclusion, arguing that the syntax should be read as referring to one figure with multiple functions. On this, see, e.g., Robert B. Laurin, "The Problem of Two Messiahs in the Qumran Scrolls," *RevQ* 4.1 (1963): 39–52; and L. D. Hurst, "Did Qumran Expect Two Messiahs?," *BBR* 9.1 (1999): 157–80, among others. The observation that there are two distinct messianic figures in CD 7:17–21 (i.e., the "scepter" and the "star") has been used against those who suggest that other messianic texts in the Damascus Document picture only one messiah.

25. Excerpts from the Dead Sea Scrolls are taken from *The Dead Sea Scrolls Translated: The Qumran Texts in English*, ed. Florentino Garcia Martinez (Leiden: Brill; Grand Rapids: Eerdmans, 1996).

These shall escape in the age of visitation; but those that remain shall be delivered up to the sword when there comes the messiah [Hebrew: *mashiach*] of Aaron and Israel. (CD 19:10–11)

And thus all the men who entered the new covenant . . . and turned and betrayed . . . shall not be counted in the assembly . . . until there arises the messiah [Hebrew: *mashiach*] of Aaron and Israel. (CD 19:33–20:1)

John Collins notes that there is "impressive evidence that the Dead Sea sect expected two messiahs, *one royal and one priestly*," which had "its biblical precedent in Zechariah's 'two sons of oil,'" and "can be traced further back, to the roles of king and High Priest in the preexilic community, and even to Moses and Aaron in the Pentateuch."[26] The royal Messiah in this construction is patterned after the expectation of a Davidic king.

Another important text for understanding the messianic teaching of the Damascus Document is 7:17–21, which does not use the word *maschiach* but mentions two messianic figures, the "scepter" and the "star." For our purposes, it is critical that the "scepter" is regarded as a militant figure. Commenting on the rise of an expectation that pictured two messiahs rather than one, Collins points to the historical circumstances surrounding the writing of these texts:

The revival of messianic expectation in the Hasmonean era represented a critique of the Jewish rulers of the day. Some traditionalists deemed them illegitimate kings because they were not from the line of David. Others also objected to

---

26. Collins, *The Scepter and the Star*, 77 (emphasis added).

their combination of the offices of high priest and king. The messianic expectations represented the dissidents' view of the proper order of society. In the Psalms of Solomon, the emphasis is on Davidic lineage. In the sectarian scrolls, the emphasis is on the separation of offices of priest and king.[27]

As with the texts we have already examined, these texts express concerns over (1) the legitimacy of those ruling over Israel and (2) the need for Davidic descent to remain at the forefront of the messianic expectations. As mentioned above, our Dead Sea texts represent a fraction of the references to Messiah in that corpus of writings. About these texts, Collins concludes:

> The portrait of the ideal king that emerges from this corpus is sketchy but consistent. He is the scepter who will smite the nations, slay the wicked with the breath of his lips, and restore the Davidic dynasty. . . . He is also the messiah of righteousness, who will usher in an era of peace and justice. He is presumably a human figure, although he is endowed with the spirit of the Lord. He is expected to restore a dynasty rather than rule forever himself.[28]

When we look at messianic ideas from these Dead Sea Scrolls against the backdrop of our previous two examples (Psalms of Solomon, 1 Enoch) we find a picture that is considerably more complex. Still, we are able to identify and extract some common elements of the visions of Messiah. First, we again find an emphasis on the royal functions of (at least one) Messiah and his Davidic pedigree. Second, Messiahs are sent by God and anointed by God's spirit. Third, the spirit-led,

---

27. John J. Collins, *Apocalypticism in the Dead Sea Scrolls* (London and New York: Routledge, 1997), 79.

28. Collins, *The Scepter and the Star*, 67.

royal-Davidic Messiah comes for the purpose of waging war against the enemies of God and God's people.

While the foregoing represents only a portion of the Second Temple Jewish literature devoted to discussing and anticipating the arrival of a messianic figure, our survey provides us with a broader context to evaluate further Mark's understanding of Messiah. For now, we are positioned to uncover common elements of messianic expectation that Mark shares with the texts we have examined. We will also note elements that Mark has altered or abandoned altogether.

WHAT DOES MARK MEAN BY MESSIAH?

While recognizing their differences—and without oversimplifying the nuances of the literature surveyed above—we have identified at least four common elements appearing alongside one another in some of the important messianic texts of the Second Temple period: an expectation of (1) Davidic descent, (2) anointment by God, (3) the presence of God's spirit, and (4) an anticipation of militancy against the illegitimate kings ruling over Israel. Below we will see that Mark has retained these elements though he modifies and molds them into his own distinctive portrait. I must emphasize that we cannot establish Mark's awareness of or literary dependence on *any of the texts examined above*, though we find hints of the same type of messianic elements within Mark, and in some cases, hovering below the surface of the narrative. Whether drawing on specific texts or capitalizing on common elements of messianic expectation, Mark's vision of Messiah both significantly overlaps with the various messianic depictions during his period as well as forges its own distinctive contours. We consider these below.

1. Is Mark's Jesus the "Son of David"?

Does Mark understand Jesus to be the "Son of David"? While Mark does not attempt to establish this by referring to a genealogy of Jesus, he does appear to have a Son of David Christology. Unlike the other Synoptic Gospels, Mark tells us nothing of Jesus's lineage or family background before he arrives on the scene to be baptized by John the Baptist. Mark will later mention the family of Jesus (3:21–34; 6:3), but he does not identify the family members as descendants of David. By contrast, Matthew's Gospel begins with the declaration that Jesus is the "son of David, son of Abraham" (1:1), and then devotes a great deal of narrative space to developing this theme. Matthew mentions David seventeen times and is clearly concerned to demonstrate that Jesus is the Son of David, both by genealogical descent and behavior.

Luke refers to David twelve times and, like Matthew, provides a genealogy that traces Jesus's lineage directly through David (Luke 3:23–38). Mark, however, makes no such explicit connection to a Davidic lineage and mentions David only seven times (2:25; 10:47, 48; 11:10; 12:35, 36, 37). Further, the phrase "Son of David," appears only twice in Mark (see 10:46–52; 12:35–37) and in neither instance is it connected to Jesus's lineage. Given this paucity of evidence—especially when compared to the more robust presentations in Matthew and Luke—is it likely that *Mark* regards Jesus as the "Son of David"?[29]

Remember that one of our core principles is that we must let Mark be Mark. If we choose to study Mark as a narrative

---

29. In his recent book on this subject, Max Botner argues that we must understand Mark's more subtle sociolinguistic framework and leveraging of Scriptures from the Hebrew Bible at various turns in the ministry of the Markan Jesus. See Max Botner, *Jesus Christ as the Son of David in the Gospel of Mark*, SNTSMS 74 (Cambridge, UK: Cambridge University Press, 2019).

apart from other versions of Jesus, we are not compelled to give greater weight to later and more explicit texts such as Matthew and Luke—both of whom made generous use of Mark's text and appear to have intentionally developed the picture of Jesus's Davidic lineage. In other words, just because Mark is not as direct or explicit on this question as later writings, it does not lead to the conclusion that he has no understanding of Jesus as the Son of David. Approaching the text of Mark in this way allows us to uncover a subtle but important emphasis on Jesus as Davidic Messiah.

If we begin by looking at Mark's uses of the title, we note that in 10:46–52, blind Bartimaeus explicitly refers to Jesus as "Son of David" when approaching him with a request to have his vision restored:

> They came to Jericho. As he and his disciples and a large crowd were leaving Jericho, Bartimaeus son of Timaeus, a blind beggar, was sitting by the roadside. When he heard that it was Jesus of Nazareth, he began to shout out and say, "Jesus, Son of David, have mercy on me!" Many sternly ordered him to be quiet, but he cried out even more loudly, "Son of David, have mercy on me!" Jesus stood still and said, "Call him here." And they called the blind man, saying to him, "Take heart; get up, he is calling you." So throwing off his cloak, he sprang up and came to Jesus. Then Jesus said to him, "What do you want me to do for you?" The blind man said to him, "My teacher, let me see again." Jesus said to him, "Go; your faith has made you well." Immediately he regained his sight and followed him on the way. (10:46–52)

In this context, Jesus neither silences Bartimaeus nor corrects him, but responds by granting his request. This response represents a tacit acceptance by Jesus that the title ascribed to him by Bartimaeus is valid. About this text, Donald Juel insightfully comments that:

> The "confession" of blind Bartimaeus in 10:47 suggests rather that the title "son of David" is appropriate for Jesus: *the blind man sees what Jesus' disciples (and authorities) cannot.* To argue that Jesus could accept the designation "Christ, the Son of the Blessed" from the high priest (Mark 14:61–62) while insisting two chapters earlier that Christ is not the "son of David" is improbable, whether we are considering the actual words of Jesus or Mark's story world.[30]

This passage provides us with a full-bodied understanding of Mark's vision of Jesus's Davidic status.[31] The other figures identified as Son of David in the Second Temple literature surveyed above are not pictured as possessing miraculous capabilities. While they operate under the power of God's spirit, they do not come with the ability or authority to perform deeds of power such as Jesus displays here.[32] As the Markan Son of David, Jesus is distinctive in this way.

---

30. Donald Juel, *Messianic Exegesis: Christological Interpretation of the Old Testament in Early Christianity* (Philadelphia: Fortress, 1988), 142 (emphasis added).

31. It is important to note that not every scholar agrees with my reading here. Important scholars such as Elizabeth Struthers Malbon (*Mark's Jesus: Characterization as Narrative Christology* [Waco, TX: Baylor University Press, 2009]) and Eugene Boring (*Mark: A Commentary*, NTL [Louisville: Westminster John Knox, 2006]) argue that Mark rejects this title. On the history of this discussion, see Max Botner, "What Has Mark's Christ to Do with David's Son? A History of Interpretation," *CurBR* 16.1 (2017): 50–70.

32. Although Michael R. Whitenton (*Hearing Kyriotic Sonship: A Cognitive and Rhetorical Approach to the Characterization of Mark's Jesus*, BibInt 148 [Leiden: Brill, 2016], 214–16) argues that Solomon, the literal son of David, is associated with therapeutic capabilities in *Test. Sol.* 20.1. See also Max Botner, "The Messiah is 'the Holy One': *ho hagios tou theou* as a Messianic Title in Mark 1:24," *JBL* 136.2 (2017): 417–33.

Matthew Novenson has written that messiahs in the ancient world could be "born"—that is, they were understood to be messiah by biological descent—or they could be "made"—that is, appointed and confirmed messiah irrespective of lineage.[33] In the Bartimaeus episode, we can see that for Mark, Jesus is the Son of David by virtue of his mission and the paradigmatic behavior that characterizes his public ministry: teaching, healing, casting out demons. Mark, however, makes no attempt to establish Jesus as hailing from a Davidic lineage, and this is a critical point of departure from the other messianic expectations we have surveyed. In this way, we might describe Mark's Jesus as "functionally Davidic," since Mark has made no attempt to establish a formal line of Davidic descent. In other words, Jesus is the messianic descendant of David because he acts as David's son more than he descends from David (again we see the probable influence of Psalm 2 here).

A second component to being identified as a Davidic Messiah is having royal status. During his triumphal entry into Jerusalem, Jesus is welcomed as the one who is ushering in a new Davidic reign:

> Many people spread their cloaks on the road, and others spread leafy branches that they had cut in the fields. Then those who went ahead and those who followed were shouting,
>
> "Hosanna!
>   Blessed is the one who comes in the name of the
>   Lord!

---

33. See the chapter "Messiahs Born and Made" in Novenson, *Grammar of Messianism*, 65–113.

> Blessed is the coming kingdom of our ancestor
> David!
> Hosanna in the highest heaven!" (Mark 11:9–10)

This acclamation represents an important moment for the audience. The narrator identified Jesus as the Messiah from the Gospel's opening verse, and now we see a public acknowledgement of this status, even if those acclaiming Jesus as king possess an incomplete understanding of his messianic agenda. Further, throughout Mark 15 there is a consistent emphasis on Jesus's kingship. By now, the literary audience knows that Jesus is the "King of the Jews" despite the skeptical questioning (15:2) and mocking (15:9, 18–20, 26, 31) he receives. While dripping with irony, these scenes are designed to confirm Jesus's royal-messianic status despite a ministry that appears to be both nonroyal and non-messianic.

Still more can be gleaned from a careful analysis of Mark's narrative. In his recent book, *Jesus Christ as the Son of David in the Gospel of Mark*, Max Botner demonstrates that Mark draws an undeniable connection between Jesus and David by introducing and building on the imagery of royal psalms (e.g., Pss 2, 110, 118) at critical points in Jesus's ministry, including the baptism (1:9–11), first passion prediction (8:31–33), transfiguration (9:2–13), triumphal entry (11:1–11), and Jesus's trial before the Sanhedrin (14:53–65). Mark's use of Scriptural references throughout the major moments of Jesus's ministry suggests that he "read Davidic superscriptions in the Psalter as an invitation to fuse the 'past King David with the future Messiah.'"[34] Again, while this presentation of Jesus is more subtle and requires nuance

---

34. Botner, *Jesus Christ as the Son of David in the Gospel of Mark*, 60–61.

to articulate, there is nevertheless strong evidence to suggest that Mark had a profound vision of Jesus as the Son of David.

Does Mark understand Jesus to be the Son of David? To this question we must answer yes, but in a distinctive way that departs from the model of other Son of David texts that anticipate a biological descendant of David, and certainly in a manner different from later NT writers. For Mark, Jesus is the functional Son of David by virtue of his calling, mission, and paradigmatic behavior. His ironic acclamation as king— despite the circumstances that suggest he is not—punctuates Mark's emphasis on Jesus as the royal, Davidic Messiah.

2. Has Mark's Jesus Been Authorized/Sent by God?

The specific language of "sending" or being "sent by God," while common elsewhere in the NT, is not prominent in Mark. Nevertheless, this *theme* is present even if the specific language that denotes it is not. Scholars have often noted that God rarely appears directly in Mark's Gospel, even though God plays a prominent role in the unfolding drama.[35] The literary audience hears the voice of God on two separate occasions—once at the baptism (1:11) and again at the transfiguration (9:7). In both instances God affirms that Jesus is his Son—in the first text expressing his pleasure with Jesus, and in the second commanding those present to listen to him. As we trace the unfolding narrative rhetoric across the whole Gospel, we find sufficient evidence to conclude that God has sent Jesus and sanctioned his mission. Thus, in response to the question, "Has Mark's Jesus been authorized/ sent by God?," the unqualified answer is yes.

---

35. For a helpful presentation of the role of God in Mark, see Ira Brent Driggers, *Following God Through Mark: Theological Tension in the Second Gospel* (Louisville: Westminster John Knox, 2007).

3. Is Mark's Jesus Endowed with God's Spirit?

God's Spirit makes an appearance early in the drama and continues to guide Jesus throughout. In his early testimony, John the Baptist has already proclaimed that Jesus will baptize with the Spirit (1:8). Then, during Jesus's baptism, the Spirit descends on him as a dove as the voice of God proclaims that Jesus is God's Son (1:10–11). Following this, the Spirit immediately guides Jesus into the wilderness, though we notice that the language describing the Spirit's leading is not mild (1:12). Rather, we read that the Spirit "drove" or "thrust" (Greek: *ekballō*) Jesus into the wilderness. To get a better feel for this image, it might be helpful to picture a hard, two-handed shove in the back. As Jesus returns from the wilderness and engages in his public ministry, the presence of the Spirit is the force that enables Jesus to preach with power (3:23–27; 4:1–9, 21–34; 12:1–9; 13:28–31), cast out demons (1:21–28; 3:11–12; 5:1–20), and perform miracles and other deeds of power (1:29–34, 40–45; 2:1–12; 3:1–6; 5:21–43; 6:53–56; 7:24–30, 31–37; 8:22–26; 9:14–29; 10:46–52). Mark leaves little doubt that Jesus has been endowed with God's Spirit to do God's work on earth.

4. Has Mark's Jesus Come to Wage War?

Despite the presence of the first three messianic elements discussed above, scholars have often referred to Jesus's ministry in Mark as having a "non-messianic" character. Some of that is likely due to the way we must answer the present question: Has Mark's Jesus come to wage war against the corrupt kings ruling over Israel? When posed in this way, the answer to this question is clearly no. Along with Jesus's death at the hands of the Romans—which suggests that he was, at the very least, *a failed Messiah*—the fact that Jesus executes his messianic vocation in a nonmilitant way is Mark's most

significant departure from common conceptions of Messiah.
If we alter the question slightly, however, our answer changes
and this will allow us a clearer vision of Mark's understanding
of Messiah.

Has Mark's Jesus come for the purpose of waging a war?
Yes. While he has not come to wage war against the illegitimate ruling kings over Israel, he has come to wage a war
against Satanic forces in the spiritual realm. Within the
Gospel's apocalyptic framework, we witness a battle between
God and Satan that is already raging when Jesus enters the
scene in Mark 1. Jesus becomes God's representative in this
battle and possesses both the authority and the power to wage
(and ultimately win) that war. When Jesus is thrust into the
wilderness to be tempted by Satan for forty days, he not only
survives the encounter, but Mark notes that he was "with the
wild beasts and the angels waited on him" (1:13). This vision
of Jesus with the wild beasts constitutes a reversal of the circumstances in the garden of Eden after the fall. Jesus, in
this initial power encounter with Satan, begins the process of
vanquishing his foe. The fruits of this victory will be seen over
and over again throughout the Gospel as Jesus easily casts
out unclean spirits, heals the infirm, and even raises a little
girl from the dead. The Markan Jesus has certainly come to
wage a war, but not in the way expressed by many, if not most,
messianic expectations of the time.

MARK'S DISTINCTIVE VISION OF MESSIAH

As mentioned at the outset of this chapter, Mark opens his
narrative with the announcement that Jesus is the Christ.
For Mark, it is critical that his readers understand both *that*
and *how* Jesus is Messiah. If we are going to appreciate the
Gospel and its distinctive contributions to early Christianity,

we must wrestle with this important theme. Jesus is the Messiah/Christ. What does this mean? I have argued that Mark's vision of a Messiah, while consistent with some aspects of other messianic expectations reflected in Second Temple literature, was also distinctive. Having examined both the Second Temple literature proximate to Mark's Gospel and the narrative itself, we are now in a position to articulate an understanding of what Mark means when he refers to Jesus as the Messiah.

For Mark, Jesus has been sent by God and endowed with God's spirit to wage war, not against wicked kings, but against the powers of Satan in the spiritual realm. He is unique in that his implements of war are exorcisms, miracles, and other deeds of power. His victory in this war is secured through his initial encounter with Satan in the wilderness, but it will ultimately be realized through his service to humanity via his sacrificial death and resurrection (10:45). He proves by virtue of his calling and paradigmatic behavior to be the functional Son of David and thus a king. The circumstances surrounding his condemnation and death will serve as the ironic means by which his royal status is confirmed. Jesus will bring his messianic mission to completion by means of his resurrection from the dead. As we consider other themes in Mark, this is the understanding of Messiah that will guide our deliberations.

FOR FURTHER READING

A. *The Text-Critical Issue in 1:1*

Ehrman, Bart D. "The Text of Mark in the Hands of the Orthodox." *LQ* 5.2 (1991): 149–52.

Head, Peter. "A Text-Critical Study of Mark 1.1 'The Beginning of the Gospel of Jesus Christ.'" *NTS* 37.4 (1991): 621–29.

Wasserman, Tommy. "The 'Son of God' Was in the Beginning
    (Mark 1:1)." *JTS* 62.1 (2011): 20–50.

B. Christology in Mark

Kingsbury, Jack Dean. *The Christology of Mark's Gospel.*
    Philadelphia: Fortress, 1983.
Le Donne, Anthony, ed. *Christology in Mark's Gospel: Four Views.*
    Critical Points Series. Grand Rapids: Zondervan Academic,
    2021.
Malbon, Elizabeth Struthers. *Mark's Jesus: Characterization as
    Narrative Christology.* Waco, TX: Baylor University Press, 2009.

C. Messiah/Messianism and Mark

Botner, Max. *Jesus Christ as the Son of David in the Gospel of Mark.*
    SNTSMS 174. Cambridge, UK: Cambridge University Press,
    2019.
Collins, John J. *The Scepter and the Star: The Messiahs of the Dead
    Sea Scrolls and Other Ancient Literature.* ABRL. New York:
    Doubleday, 1995.
Jipp, Joshua W. *The Messianic Theology of the New Testament.* Grand
    Rapids: Eerdmans, 2020.
Juel, Donald. *Messianic Exegesis: Christological Interpretation of the
    Old Testament in Early Christianity.* Philadelphia: Fortress, 1988.
Novenson, Matthew V. *The Grammar of Messianism: An Ancient
    Jewish Political Idiom and Its Users.* Oxford: Oxford University
    Press, 2017.
Yarbro Collins, Adela, and John J. Collins. *King and Messiah as Son
    of God: Divine, Human, and Angelic Messianic Figures in Biblical
    and Related Literature.* Grand Rapids: Eerdmans, 2008.

D. Other Ancient Literature Discussed in This Chapter

Psalms of Solomon

Atkinson, Kenneth. *I Cried to the Lord: A Study of the Psalms of
    Solomon's Historical Background and Social Setting.* JSJSup 84.
    Leiden: Brill, 2004.
Bons, Eberhard, and Patrick Pouchelle, eds. *The Psalms of Solomon:
    Language, History, Theology.* EJL 40. Atlanta: SBL Press, 2015.

Wright, Robert B., ed. *The Psalms of Solomon: A Critical Addition of the Greek Text.* Jewish and Christian Texts in Context and Related Studies 1. London: T&T Clark, 2007.

1 Enoch

Isaac, Ephraim. "1 Enoch." In *The Old Testament Pseudepigrapha,* vol. 1. Edited by James H. Charlesworth, 3–89. ABRL. New York: Doubleday, 1983.

Nickelsburg, George W. E., and James C. VanderKam. *1 Enoch 2: A Commentary on 1 Enoch Chapters 37–82.* Hermeneia. Minneapolis: Fortress, 2012.

Stuckenbruck, Loren, and Gabriele Boccaccini, eds. *Enoch and the Synoptic Gospels: Reminiscences, Allusions, Intertextuality.* EJL 44. Atlanta: SBL Press, 2016.

Dead Sea Scrolls

Collins, John J. *Apocalypticism in the Dead Sea Scrolls.* London: Routledge, 1997.

Fitzmyer, Joseph A. *The Dead Sea Scrolls and Christian Origins.* Studies in the Dead Sea Scrolls and Related Literature. Grand Rapids: Eerdmans, 2000.

Garcia Martinez, Florentino, ed. *The Dead Sea Scrolls Translated: The Qumran Texts in English.* Leiden: Brill; Grand Rapids: Eerdmans, 1996.

CHAPTER 4

"Who Is This Man?" (Part 2)

Jesus the Son of God

In this chapter, we will continue examining the major theme of Jesus's identity in Mark. Now we turn to the second title in Mark's programmatic description of Jesus in the Gospel's opening verse: the Son of God (Greek: *ho huios tou theou*). In the previous chapter, we observed that many contemporary readers of the NT misunderstand how the title Messiah functioned in its ancient contexts. The same is true for the title Son of God. Some well-intentioned readers will assume that whenever the title appears in the NT it refers to Jesus as the second person of the Holy Trinity. Other readers insist that the title is an indication of Jesus's divine status. I have often heard students assert that Jesus is both divine and human, and that the title Son of God alerts us to his divinity, while the title Son of Man is an affirmation of his humanity.[1] We must remember that there is no one-to-one correspondence between the ideas and images in our biblical texts and

---

1. This formulation misunderstands both titles and ultimately relies on a much later doctrinal formulation known as the Chalcedonian Definition (451 CE). Here we must disentangle our understanding of Jesus, the Son of God, the second person of the Holy Trinity, from ancient conceptions and their employment in the Gospel.

later theological formulations that were developed to explain the "grand story" of the Bible to Christian audiences. This is especially true of conversations about the nature of Jesus that took place in the first five centuries of the church.[2] It is not difficult to understand why some contemporary readers of the NT approach the title Son of God in these ways, but each one fails to capture its significance in the unfolding Christology of Mark's Gospel. As in our discussion of messianic ideas in the previous chapter, we must situate the title Son of God in its ancient social, political, and religious contexts to arrive at a more faithful understanding of what Mark means when he ascribes it to Jesus. On the difficulty of this task, Lewis S. Hay notes: "The conspicuously favored position which Mark affords the title 'Son of God' has been noted by New Testament scholars for many years. . . . That Mark has a high regard for the title is not seriously questioned, *but the precise meaning of the title for the evangelist is a matter of sharp debate.*"[3] In light of this debate, the present chapter will attempt to provide a few answers to some of the bedeviling questions surrounding Mark's use of the title and further explicate how he envisions Jesus as *both* Messiah and Son of God.

While we have established that the term Messiah is self-evidently Jewish in origin and usage, this is not so clear with

---

2. For Christians within Roman Catholic, Orthodox, and Protestant traditions, the Chalcedonian Definition (451 CE) provides the orthodox understanding of Jesus: He is fully divine and fully human *at the same time*. We need to recognize, however, that the road to Chalcedon was a long and circuitous one that included numerous christological controversies (e.g., Arianism, Docetism, Monophysitism, Nestorianism, etc.) followed by ecumenical councils (e.g., Nicaea, Constantinople, Ephesus, Chalcedon) that clarified the official teaching of the church. For more on the various controversies, see David E. Wilhite, *The Gospel According to Heretics: Discovering Orthodoxy through Early Christological Conflicts* (Grand Rapids: Baker Academic, 2015).

3. Lewis S. Hay, "The Son-of-God Christology in Mark," *JBR* 32.2 (1964): 106–14 (here 106; emphasis added).

the designation Son of God—at least not as it is used in the Second Gospel. Adam Winn has recently argued that in Mark, one of the most fruitful ways of understanding Messiah is in the context of Roman anti-imperial rhetoric. He further argues that both titles are perhaps best understood against the backdrop of events that took place during the rule of the Roman emperor Vespasian. Winn makes this claim in part by conflating Mark's use of the terms Messiah (Greek: *christos*), Son of God (Greek: *ho huios tou theou*), and Son of Man (Greek: *ho huios tou anthrōpou*). He notes, "That Mark can use 'Messiah,' 'Son of God,' and 'Son of Man' to reference Jesus' messianic identity, with no explanation given to the reader, strongly suggests the reader already *understood these terms as virtual synonyms*."[4] While I agree that Mark's depiction of Jesus is, in part, meant to interact with Roman imperial propaganda, especially depictions of Caesar as the Son of God, I believe Winn goes too far in conflating these three titles. More balanced is the view of Adela Yarbro Collins, who recognizes that Mark's Christology would have communicated certain ideas to Jewish readers but that non-Jewish Roman readers were likely to understand them "differently from those who preferred or were unconsciously shaped by certain Jewish traditions."[5] The discussion in this chapter will attempt to show how Mark capitalizes on both Jewish and Roman concepts in applying the language of divine sonship to Jesus. It is incumbent on us, therefore, to understand how the title was employed within both contexts. We will find that the acclamation of Jesus as the Son

---

4. Adam Winn, *Reading Mark's Christology Under Caesar: Jesus the Messiah and Roman Imperial Ideology* (Downers Grove: IVP Academic, 2019), 61 (emphasis added).

5. Adela Yarbro Collins, "Mark and His Readers: The Son of God among Greeks and Romans," *HTR* 93.3 (2000): 85–100 (here 87).

of God signals different things in different places within the narrative and, likewise, could have (and likely *would have*) communicated different things to different audiences in the first-century Roman world.

JEWISH CONCEPTIONS OF THE SON OF GOD

We begin with the observation that "Son of God" (Hebrew: *ben haElohim*) was applied to numerous individuals and groups within both the Hebrew Bible and the literature of Second Temple Judaism. In some instances, the Hebrew title does not necessarily refer to a son or descendant at all. On this, Kratz notes that the title can be "a generic term and means nothing but 'god' in the same way that 'son of man' (*ben adam*) is 'man' and 'son of an ox' (*ben baqar*) is 'ox.'"[6] This means that the title in itself does not always describe the relationship between a father and son but expresses something about the divine nature of an earthly or heavenly figure.[7] Further, in the Hebrew Bible, the title "son of God" is applied to the mysterious Nephilim (Gen 6:2–4), the nation of Israel (e.g., Exod 4:22), kings (e.g., 2 Sam 7:14; 1 Chr 22:10; 28:6), and even angels (e.g., Job 1:6; 2:1; 38:7). Thus, it should be clear that designating something or someone as a "son of God" in many of these contexts is not the same as assigning them a status of ontological divinity. Rather, the title is used variously to emphasize something unique about an individual or group, to underscore God's affection for them, or even to set them apart as God's representative.

---

6. Reinhard G. Kratz, "Son of God and Son of Man: 4Q246 in the Light of the Book of Daniel," in *Son of God: Divine Sonship in Jewish and Christian Antiquity*, ed. Garrick V. Allen, Kai Akagi, Paul Sloan, and Madhavi Nevader (State College, PA: Pennsylvania State University Press, 2019), 9.

7. Kratz, "Son of God and Son of Man," 9.

In Jewish writings of the Second Temple period, divine sonship is treated with equal variety. For example, in the Jewish novel *Joseph and Aseneth* (written in Greek, ca. 200 BCE–200 CE), which is an expansion of material found in Gen 41, the patriarch Joseph is referred to both as "the son of God" (6:3, 5) and as God's "firstborn" son (Greek: *prōtotokos*; 21:4).[8] The story of Joseph and Aseneth is partially intended to remind its readers of the rivalry and conflict that existed between Israel and Egypt in the exodus, where the death of the firstborn is a particularly important theme. The references to Joseph as God's son and especially "firstborn" son contrast with the death of Pharoah's "firstborn." They are also likely meant to emphasize the superiority of Israel as well as Joseph's role as "true" firstborn son and thus victor in Israel-Egypt conflicts.[9]

Similarly, in the Prayer of Joseph—an expansion of Gen 48–49 (likely composed in Aramaic in the first century CE)—both Joseph and the angel Uriel are referred to as "sons of God." This appellation is clearly used as a synonym for "angel."[10] We also see references to pious men as "sons of God" in the first-century BCE text Wisdom of Solomon (2:13–18; 5:5) as well as the second-century BCE text Wisdom of Ben Sira (4:10).

More interesting, and perhaps even more pertinent for our study of Mark, we find numerous Second Temple texts

---

8. For an accessible English translation, see David Cook, "Joseph and Aseneth," in H. F. D. Sparks, *The Apocryphal Old Testament* (Oxford: Oxford University Press, 1984), 465–504.

9. For more on this, see Kyu Seop Kim, "The Meaning of the Firstborn Son in Joseph and Aseneth," *JSJ* 49 (2018), 404–16.

10. See J. Z. Smith, "The Prayer of Joseph," in *The Old Testament Pseudepigrapha*, ed. James H. Charlesworth, vol. 2, ABRL (New York: Doubleday, 1983), 699–714.

applying the title of God's son to *the Messiah*. Among the most important of these is 4Q246, the so-called Son of God text from Qumran, likely written in Aramaic in the second century BCE. There we read, "The prince of nations [will arise].... He will be called the son of God. And the son of the Most High God they will call him.... The sword will cease from the land. And all the nations shall do homage to him there."[11]

This brief and incomplete review of Jewish texts reveals that there is no unanimity of meaning with which the term "son of God" is applied in the Hebrew Bible or Second Temple literature. In fact, there are so many variations that it is difficult to put them into discrete categories. Practically, this means that we cannot make immediate assumptions about what Mark means when he uses the title throughout the Gospel. As always, we must be careful to trace the developing narrative rhetoric within the text while remaining sensitive to what may lie in the background.

It is not totally clear what Mark intends by the title *just from an analysis of the Jewish literature of the period*, though as with our discussion of Messiah above, we see that the language and imagery of Psalm 2 remain important. In 1:11, Mark quotes, or at least strongly alludes to the language of Ps 2:7 ("You are my son").[12] He then appears to map the movements of the psalm onto the unfolding scenes in 1:9–15. On this, Joel Marcus perceptively notes:

---

11. Translation from Edward M. Cook, "4Q246," *BBR* 5.1 (1993): 43–66 (here 47).

12. Joel Marcus (*Mark 1–8: A New Translation with Introduction and Commentary*, AB 27 (New York: Doubleday, 2000, 162), notes that, "This is a near-exact quotation of Ps 2:7 LXX, the only difference being that the psalm verse puts the predicate nominative first ('my son are you')."

Mark's use of Psalm 2, then, is not limited to the direct
citation of it in 1:1. Rather the whole series of pericopes
in 1:9–11, 12–13, 14–15 reflects the basic 'plot' of the
psalm, and its influence may extend further into Mark's
story. The enemy forces, concretizations of primeval
chaos, array themselves against the Lord and against his
anointed, shouting in defiance, 'What have you to do
with us?' (see Mark 1:24) and throwing against them all
their hostile might (see Ps. 2:1–3). The one enthroned
in heaven, however, shrugs off this display of impotent
rage and majestically brings forth his earthly executive,
an executive whose purpose and power are so deeply
congruent with his own that he can be called his son,
and that the revelation of his kingship can simultaneously
represent the earthly manifestation of the kingly power of
God (see Ps. 2:4–7).[13]

This is important context, and it will set the stage for our
reading of Mark's treatment of the term Son of God. For
now we can conclude that (1) Mark uses the title in a way
that draws on some ideas from the Hebrew Bible and Second
Temple Judaism—most notably Psalm 2, (2) the title signals
that Jesus is a unique figure in God's economy of salvation—we will see that he is the one ushering in the reign
of God (Mark 1:14–15), and (3) the title explains or further
advances our understanding of Jesus as Messiah. We must
keep all of this in mind as we approach the various texts in
which the title is applied to Jesus. Before we examine those
texts, however, it is necessary to explore the potential Roman
influences informing Mark's Christology.

---

13. Joel Marcus, *The Way of the Lord: Christological Exegesis of the Old Testament
in the Gospel of Mark* (London: T&T Clark, 1992), 68–69.

THE SON OF GOD IN ROMAN IMPERIAL PROPAGANDA

Over the past few decades, scholars of early Christianity have devoted much attention to the historical and cultural background of the Roman Empire and its impact on the NT writers. We cannot escape the observation that the authors of the NT texts were writing under Roman rule and that the everyday trappings of the empire were pervasive and inescapable. While much of the emphasis on anti-imperial rhetoric in the NT has focused on the letters of Paul, Revelation, and the Gospel of Matthew, scholars have increasingly recognized this undercurrent in the Gospel of Mark.[14]

One important claim arising from this scholarship is that early Christian proclamations of Jesus as "Lord," "Savior," and "Son of God" were a direct affront to claims made in Roman imperial propaganda about the deification of the emperors. For instance, we know that both Nero (54–68) and Domitian (81–96) insisted on being called "lord" (Greek: *kyrios*) and that Vespasian (69–79) was referred to as both benefactor (Greek: *euergetēs*) and savior (Greek: *sōtēr*). Upon his death, Julius Caesar was declared divine, and his adopted son, Octavius, became Augustus Caesar, "the son of [a] God" (Latin: *divi filius*; Greek: *huios theou*). This title subsequently became an important part of Roman imperial propaganda surrounding the honors due to the emperor.[15] On the phenomenon that led the Romans to think that Julius Caesar was divine, the Roman historian Suetonius notes:

---

14. See Judith Diehl, "Anti-Imperial Rhetoric in the New Testament," *CurBR* 10.1 (2011): 9–52.

15. For a substantive treatment of the title "son of God" within Mark's sociocultural context, see Michael Peppard, *The Son of God in the Roman World: Divine Sonship in Its Social and Political Context* (Oxford: Oxford University Press, 2011), 86–130.

[Julius] died in the fifty-sixth year of his age, and was numbered among the gods, not only by a formal decree, but also in the conviction of the common people. For at the first of the games which his heir Augustus gave in honour of his apotheosis, *a comet shone for seven successive days, rising about the eleventh hour and was believed to be the soul of Caesar,* who had been taken to heaven; and this is why a star is set upon the crown of his head in his statue.[16]

Augustus used the occasion of this celestial phenomenon—sometimes referred to as the "Caesar Comet"—to declare that the soul of Julius Caesar had, indeed, ascended to the gods.[17] And if his father was divine, that made Augustus a son of God. It is difficult to imagine a scenario in which early Christian authors, including Mark, applied this specific title to Jesus without appreciating its significance within the broader Roman Empire. There is, of course, ongoing debate among Markan scholars as to how pervasive these ideas are in the background of the Second Gospel. However, by the time we reach the centurion's confession, "Truly this man was God's Son," (15:39; see more on this below), it is undeniable that Mark is tapping into some of this influence. Mark poses a conspicuous challenge to the Roman imperial cult in the centurion's confession for early readers of the Gospel "because not only did the name echo the language of Roman emperor worship but it also directly challenged the most revered figure of the cult—the emperor Augustus himself."[18]

---

16. Suetonius, *Lives of the Caesars, Volume I: Julius. Augustus. Tiberius. Gaius. Caligula.*, trans. J. C. Rolfe, LCL 31 (Cambridge: Harvard University Press, 1914), 147 (emphasis added). Augustus's own account of this event is preserved in Pliny's *Naturalis Historia* 2.23.94.

17. For further context, see Robert Gurval, "Caesar's Comet: The Politics and Poetics of an Augustan Myth," *MAAR* 42.1 (1997): 39–71.

18. Tae Hun Kim, "The Anarthrous *huios theou* in Mark 15,39 and the Roman Imperial Cult," *Bib* 79.2 (1998): 221–41 (here 240).

Beyond the explicit use of son of God language in Roman imperial propaganda, scholars have also noted important connections between the language of Mark 1:1 and the Priene Calendar Inscription in honor of Augustus Caesar (ca. 9 BCE). That inscription reads in part:

> Caesar, by his appearance (excelled even our anticipations), surpassing all previous benefactors, and not even leaving to posterity any hope of surpassing what he has done, and since the birthday of the god Augustus was the beginning [Greek: *ērxen*] of the good tidings [Greek: *euangelia*] for the world that came by reason of him.[19]

We should note three critical links between these texts: First, both refer to "good news" or "glad tidings." The Greek term *euangelion*—usually rendered "gospel" in our early Christian writings—appears in both texts. Second, there is a reference to the "beginning" of this good news—Mark uses the noun form (Greek: *archē*), while the inscription uses the verbal form (Greek: *ērxen*). And third, in both instances, the "good news" is brought about by the divine agent being acclaimed.[20] After a detailed examination of the similarities between these texts in their respective contexts, Evans concludes that "Mark's purpose is to narrate the story of Jesus in such a way that such a confession will appear *compelling and plausible to Jews and Romans alike.*"[21] This is a conclusion with which I strongly agree, and I will attempt to support it below.

This brief examination of different ideological angles

---

19. Translation from Craig Evans, "Mark's Incipit and the Priene Calendar Inscription: From Jewish Gospel to Greco-Roman Gospel," *JGRChJ* 1.1 (2000): 69.

20. Evans, "Mark's Incipit and the Priene Calendar Inscription," 69.

21. Evans, "Mark's Incipit and the Priene Calendar Inscription," 81 (emphasis added).

reveals how we must carefully approach our reading of Mark's Christology with an appreciation of the various elements arising from within both Jewish and Roman spheres. Rather than attempting a hard separation between the Jewish on one side and the Roman (or Greco-Roman) on the other, I want to acknowledge that, for real ancient readers of the text (rather than the hypothetical "implied reader" within the narrative world) it was possible to view Mark's Christology kaleidoscopically. A kaleidoscope typically has two or more mirrors tilted at angles resulting in variations of symmetrical patterns, all depending on the angle of one's vision. In a similar manner, an appreciation of the Jewish and Roman backgrounds at work in Mark allows for various visions of Jesus, and one's angle of view will, to a large degree, determine one's vision of the text.[22] But all of this is tricky to unpack. Although it is possible that some ancient audiences were able to understand the text attuned to material from both backgrounds, it is also likely that a given reader would have been better informed by a primary frame of reference (Roman or Jewish) and may have been unable to reckon with multiple layers in the text. With all of this context in mind, we move now to a consideration of the Markan texts in which the divine sonship of Jesus is in view.

"SON OF GOD" TEXTS IN MARK

Scholars have long noted the importance of spatial designations in Mark, especially as it relates to the Sea of Galilee. Jesus and the Twelve use the sea as a way of moving back and forth between Jewish and gentile spaces. This spatial context

---

22. I am grateful to my colleague, Dr. Olivia Stewart Lester for helping me articulate this metaphor as a way of holding in tension both the Jewish and the (Greco-)Roman in Mark.

is important for situating the various texts in which the title Son of God appears in the Gospel. After the narrator's assertion in 1:1, there are eight instances in Mark's Gospel where Jesus is identified as the Son of God, six of which occur in *distinctly Jewish spaces* (1:9–11; 3:7–12; 9:2–13; 12:1–12; 13:32–37; 14:60–65). Twice the voice of God affirms that Jesus is his son, one of which is addressed to Jesus directly at his baptism in the Jordan ("You are my beloved son"; 1:11), and the other of which is addressed to three disciples who have accompanied Jesus on the Mount of Transfiguration ("This is my beloved son"; 9:7).[23] Another time the narrator reports the response of demoniacs when they encounter Jesus (3:11), and three times the title appears on the lips of Jesus—once in the context of a debate with religious leaders (12:1–12), once during the apocalyptic discourse near the Jewish temple (13:32–37), and once in his examination before the high priest (14:60–65).

The remaining two passages are set in a Roman context, one occurring on the gentile side of the Sea of Galilee (5:1–20), where Jesus comes face-to-face with a powerful demoniac, and a final one taking place at the foot of the cross (15:31–39). There we witness a Roman centurion confessing that Jesus is the Son of God. We will take up each of these texts in turn.

1. The Voice of God at the Baptism (1:9–11)

In those days Jesus came from Nazareth of Galilee and was baptized by John in the Jordan. And just as he was coming up out of the water, he saw the heavens torn apart and the Spirit descending like a dove on

---

23. Contrary to my argument here, Kelly R. Iverson (*Gentiles in the Gospel of Mark: Even the Dogs Under the Table Eat the Children's Crumbs*, LNTS 339 [London: T&T Clark, 2007], 104–25) argues that this event takes place in *gentile territory.*

him. And a voice came from heaven, "You are my Son,
the Beloved; with you I am well pleased."

This announcement is important for our developing
understanding in that it represents an early narrative confirmation that Jesus is God's Son. After the narrator's initial
declaration of Jesus (1:1), followed by an introduction to the
teaching and baptismal activity of John the Baptist (1:2–8),
we finally meet the protagonist of the story when he comes
to be baptized. Here the authoritative voice of God enters
the narrative and corroborates what the narrator asserted
in the Gospel's opening verse. We also witness the Spirit
descend on Jesus as a dove. This is an auspicious start for
Jesus as the first two authoritative voices in the text—that of
the narrator and of God—both affirm his divine sonship.
In 1:9–11 and the scenes that follow, we also begin to get an
initial sense of what it means for Jesus to be the Son of God.
Jesus's baptism represents a formal commissioning for his
public vocation. In the next scene (1:12–13), Jesus is forced
out into the wilderness and comes face-to-face with God's
chief enemy, and in that encounter he secures a proleptic
victory. This victory over Satan and his realm will continue
to have ripple effects throughout the Gospel as Jesus displays
authority in his interactions with the demonic and power over
disease and death. Then in 1:14–15, Jesus will proclaim the
arrival of God's kingdom. These opening, rapid-fire scenes
reveal critical information about what it means for Jesus to
be the Son of God.

2. The Voice of the Demoniacs in Galilee (3:11–12)

Whenever the unclean spirits saw him, they fell down
before him and shouted, "You are the Son of God!"
But he sternly ordered them not to make him known.

Throughout the Gospel of Mark, the emissaries of Satan display a clear understanding of Jesus's identity.[24] In Jesus's first interaction with an unclean spirit in 1:23–24, the demoniac confesses that he is the "Holy One of God." Below we will see another demoniac named Legion confessing that Jesus is the Son of Most High God (5:1–20). Here the narrator reports the regular habit of the unclean spirits when they come into contact with Jesus—they know he is God's Son and they openly confess that truth. In the wider context of this current text (3:7–12), Mark provides a summary of Jesus's ministry activity: a multitude of people from many regions have come out to see him (3:7–9), he has healed many of them (3:10), and he has regularly encountered unclean spirits who know who he is (3:11–12). This summary has the effect of advancing the action of the narrative while providing key information about what Jesus has experienced in his ministry to this point in the story.

3. The Voice of "Legion" in Gerasa (5:6–8)

> When he saw Jesus from a distance, he ran and bowed down before him; and he shouted at the top of his voice, "What have you to do with me, Jesus, Son of the Most High God? I adjure you by God, do not torment me." For he had said to him, "Come out of the man, you unclean spirit!"

Jesus has now entered Gerasa on the gentile side of the Sea of Galilee. Here he comes face to face with another demoniac. Earlier in the narrative Jesus told a parable about plundering

---

24. It is significant that the descent of the spirit in 1:11 accompanies the attestation that Jesus is the Son of God. Then, throughout the narrative, it is the spirits who most consistently and accurately attest to Jesus's identity. I am grateful to Paul Wheatley for this insight.

the house of the "strong man," (3:27). That parable occurs in a context where Jesus is accused by the religious leaders of casting out demons by the hand of Beelzebul. Jesus's use of strong man imagery is a transparent reference to Satan. I have argued that in his initial encounter with Satan in the wilderness (1:12–13), Jesus secured a proleptic victory in the cosmic battle that is already being waged on earth between God and Satan. While Satan is parabolically described as the strong man (Greek: *ho ischyros*), we must remember that when John the Baptist proclaimed the coming of Jesus, he announced him as the "stronger one" (1:7; literal translation of the Greek *ho ischyroteros*). Directly after John's announcement, Jesus is baptized then thrust into the wilderness for his initial showdown with Satan. When he returns after forty days, he announces the arrival of God's kingdom (1:14–15) and immediately begins providing evidence of the kingdom's arrival and his victory over Satan. This victory manifests itself partly in his ability to cast out unclean spirits with ease. Jesus, the "stronger one" has overcome Satan, "the strong man." Therefore, when this scene begins, the audience will not be concerned with the reports of this man's power or abilities (5:3–5). We are told that "no one had the strength to subdue him," (5:4), but we know that is not true. Jesus is more powerful, and this strength is immediately on display. In fact, despite reports of the man's strength, he runs directly to Jesus, falls down before him, confesses that he is "Son of the Most High God," and begs Jesus not to torture him (5:7–8). Again, the emissaries of Satan harbor no delusions about who Jesus is. They are perhaps the most consistent characters in the narrative when it comes to identifying Jesus correctly.

The man's posture before Jesus is also worth noting. The text indicates that he "bows down" before Jesus (Greek: *proskyneō*). While this word is sometimes used in contexts associated with worship, that is likely not how it is intended here. It is a posture of falling prostrate, which is a form of extreme obeisance. Given the description of the man's power and mental instability, all the elements of his immediate response to Jesus should be judged remarkable.

Commentators have noted the anti-Roman elements in this pericope, the most obvious of which is the man's name—Legion—which is a transparent reference to the largest of military units within the Roman army. That Jesus commands the "Legion" of two thousand demons to depart the man's body and allows them to enter a herd of swine (5:12), where they subsequently perish (5:13), is suggestive of Jesus's power over Rome. Jesus is not just the son of any run-of-the-mill god from the Greco-Roman pantheon. He is, as the demoniac proclaims, the Son of the Most High God and his abilities confirm this.

4. The Voice of God at the Transfiguration (9:7–8)

Then a cloud overshadowed them, and from the cloud there came a voice, "This is my Son, the Beloved; listen to him!" Suddenly when they looked around, they saw no one with them any more, but only Jesus.

The transfiguration is a climactic moment in the narrative, occurring just after Jesus's first passion prediction and discussion of the way of the cross (8:31–38). There we learn for the first time that it is necessary for Jesus to suffer, be rejected and executed, and rise again in order to fulfill the plans God has for him. We also witness Jesus's rebuke of Peter and his further explanation to the crowds of what it means to "take up one's cross" and follow. The transfiguration that follows is significant for a number of reasons.

First, on the heels of his failure to grasp the true nature

of Jesus's messianic mission, Peter (along with the other two
disciples) is addressed directly by God. As we continue to
make our way through the narrative, we will see that Peter
devolves into seemingly greater levels of incomprehension.
He is without excuse, however, because not only has he been
with Jesus and witnessed all of Jesus's teaching and miraculous activities, but he also has the very testimony of God
about the authoritative words of Jesus: "Listen to him!" God
commands.

Second, this entire scene is framed as a theophany, or a
manifestation of God's presence. The event takes place on a
mountain—an important topographical location for Mark—
and includes Moses and Elijah, both of whom also experienced the presence of God on a mountain (Exod 33:19–23;
34:4–7; 1 Kgs 19:9–11).[25] We further witness a descending
cloud, which is likely an allusion to God's presence in the "pillar of cloud" throughout the exodus (cf. Exod 13:21–22). We
must also note the important connections between this event
and an earlier scene in which Jesus walks on water in Mark
6:45–52. In 6:48, the narrator tells us that Jesus intended to
"pass . . . by" (Greek: *parerchomai*) his disciples while he was
walking on the water. This is more than simply a reference to
Jesus trying to "sneak by" the disciples. Rather, the term carries a deeper theological significance. This same Greek word
is used in the LXX theophany texts associated with Moses
and Elijah—both of whom are present in 9:2–8.

In Exod 33:19–23, God announces his intentions to pass
before (Greek: *parerchomai*, 33:19, 22) Moses and allow him to

---

25. On the importance of mountain imagery in the Second Gospel, see
Elizabeth Struthers Malbon, *Narrative Space and Mythic Meaning in Mark* (San
Francisco: Harper & Row, 1986); and, more recently, Jamie Davies, "Apocalyptic
Topography in Mark's Gospel: Theophany and Divine Invisibility at Sinai, Horeb,
and the Mount of Transfiguration," *JTI* 14.1 (2020): 140–48.

see the tail end of his glory. He subsequently hides Moses in the cleft of a rock and covers him with his hand, only removing it after he has passed. Then in Exod 34:5–8, God "passes by" Moses (Greek: *parerchomai*, 34:6), allowing him to glimpse a portion of his presence. Similarly, in 1 Kgs 19:9–10, there is a conversation between Elijah and God in which Elijah expresses his despair at being "the only one left" in service to God (19:10 NIV). In response to this, God announces that his presence is about to "pass by" (Greek: *parerchomai*, 19:11).

In Mark 6:45–52, the disciples see Jesus walking on the water and are afraid because they presume he is a ghost (6:49–50). Jesus consoles the frightened disciples with the words, "Take heart. I am. Do not be afraid." (6:50; my translation)—language that is straightforwardly connected to theophany (e.g., Gen 26:24) and the name of God in the Hebrew Bible (e.g., Exod 3:14). Commentators have long noted that this language in Mark 6 suggests something significant about Jesus's relationship to God. While the "I am" language in Mark 6 should likely not be read with the full Christological force of the same language found throughout the Fourth Gospel, it is nevertheless suggestive of a high Christology. Mark's use of "I am" (Greek: *egō eimi*) in this passage suggests an ambiguity similar to Hebrew Bible texts in which an angel or human emissary sent by God is referred to by the title of "God" (cf. Gen 16:10–13; 32:23–32).

When we examine the transfiguration in light of earlier Christological texts in Mark, and 6:45–52 in particular, we continue to see various contours of Mark's presentation of Jesus as the Son of God. First, God's command to the disciples to listen to Jesus confirms his authority as a teacher. There is thus a revelatory character to the ministry of Jesus that provides the disciples access to God. The command to listen also looks back to the previous section and confirms that

Jesus's words about his impending death are to be heeded by
the disciples.

5. The Voice of Jesus in Jerusalem, Part 1 (12:1–12)

Then he began to speak to them in parables. "A man
planted a vineyard, put a fence around it, dug a pit for
the wine press, and built a watchtower; then he leased
it to tenants and went to another country. When the
season came, he sent a slave to the tenants to collect
from them his share of the produce of the vineyard.
But they seized him, and beat him, and sent him away
empty-handed. And again he sent another slave to
them; this one they beat over the head and insulted.
Then he sent another, and that one they killed. And
so it was with many others; some they beat, and others
they killed. He had still one other, a beloved son.
Finally he sent him to them, saying, 'They will respect
my son.' But those tenants said to one another, 'This
is the heir; come, let us kill him, and the inheritance
will be ours.' So they seized him, killed him, and
threw him out of the vineyard. What then will the
owner of the vineyard do? He will come and destroy
the tenants and give the vineyard to others. Have you
not read this scripture:

'The stone that the builders rejected
    has become the cornerstone;
this was the Lord's doing,
    and it is amazing in our eyes'?"

When they realized that he had told this parable
against them, they wanted to arrest him, but they
feared the crowd. So they left him and went away.

The previous Son of God passages we have examined have been abbreviated in the interests of space. Here, however, it is important for us to see the entire passage in its context. Jesus has entered a setting that will see him face off with the religious leaders in a series of disputes across Mark 12. The controversy begins with Jesus uttering this parable about the tenants of the vineyard rejecting and killing the vineyard owner's son. The connections between the various details of this parable and the fate awaiting Jesus seem clear: God is owner of the vineyard, the religious leaders are the tenants, and Jesus is the beloved Son (cf. Gen 22:2, 12, 16) who loses his life at the hands of the impetuous tenants. Jesus has thrice predicted his rejection by the religious leaders resulting in his death (8:31; 9:31; 10:32–34). This parable adds greater historical-theological context to the circumstances surrounding his impending crucifixion. As Jesus tells it, he is the last in a long line of messengers (i.e., prophets) sent to God's people whom they have ignored in favor of their own interests. While they merely rejected the previous messengers, the religious leaders will perpetrate the ultimate indignity on the son as their rejection of him will culminate in his being "seized, killed, and thrown out of the vineyard." We cannot overlook that an essential part of what it means for Jesus to be God's Son is that he must suffer and die. Here is an element missing from the other divine son imagery we surveyed above—both within the Jewish and Roman spheres.

6. The Voice of Jesus in Jerusalem, Part 2 (13:32–33)

But about that day or hour no one knows, neither the angels in heaven, nor the Son, but only the Father. Beware, keep alert; for you do not know when the time will come.

Here Jesus affirms that the arrival of "that day"—likely a reference to the day of the Lord (cf. Isa 2:12; Amos 5:18–20)—is known only to the Father. This passing reference to "the Son" does not appear to add much to our understanding of Jesus as the divine Son in Mark. However, given later Christological developments within early Christianity, it is important to note that, in affirming his status as God's Son, the Markan Jesus indicates that he has limited knowledge of future events. This may not signal very much within the overall context of Mark's Gospel, but when we compare it with the sort of knowledge Jesus possesses in the Fourth Gospel, we notice a substantial difference. This is another instance where it is important for us to "let Mark be Mark."

7. The Voice of Jesus in Jerusalem, Part 3 (14:60–65)

Then the high priest stood up before them and asked Jesus, "Have you no answer? What is it that they testify against you?" But he was silent and did not answer. Again the high priest asked him, "Are you the Messiah, the Son of the Blessed One?" Jesus said, "I am; and

> 'you will see the Son of Man
> seated at the right hand of the Power,'
> and 'coming with the clouds of heaven.'"

Then the high priest tore his clothes and said, "Why do we still need witnesses? You have heard his blasphemy! What is your decision?" All of them condemned him as deserving death. Some began to spit on him, to blindfold him, and to strike him, saying to him, "Prophesy!" The guards also took him over and beat him.

This passage is unique in that it includes in the same space, the three major titles used for Jesus throughout Mark: Messiah, Son of God (here, "Son of the Blessed One"), and Son of Man. I suggest that the titles, to a certain degree, should be used to interpret one another. At the very least, we cannot understand what it means for Jesus to be the Messiah without also understanding what it means for him to be the Son of God. This passage also contains the most explicit admission on the part of Jesus that he is God's Son. Once again we see the use of "I am" language (14:62), which signals the presence of a high Christology. In addition to the explicit affirmation of his status as God's Son, Jesus indicates that he will (1) be seated at God's right hand and (2) arrive on the clouds of heaven. That the high priest regards these claims as blasphemous is clear from his reaction.

8. The Voice of the Centurion at the Cross (15:37–39):

Then Jesus gave a loud cry and breathed his last. And the curtain of the temple was torn in two, from top to bottom. Now when the centurion, who stood facing him, saw that in this way he breathed his last, he said, "Truly this man was God's Son!"

As mentioned above, this is the most explicitly Roman scene in the Gospel. Jesus has been given a *Roman* death sentence and is found hanging on a *Roman* cross. Witnessing Jesus's death is a *Roman* centurion who confesses: "Truly this man was God's Son!" (15:39). This proclamation has caused no little debate. Some commentators have regarded it as insincere or derisive, while others have insisted that the claim is sincere and represents a watershed moment in the narrative.[26] I am persuaded by the latter position as it better accords with the unfolding narrative rhetoric. Here Mark employs a Roman character at work in a Roman space and uses his words to signal something of theological import about Jesus. The audience already knows that Jesus is God's Son, but in this moment, his status emerges in a new and different way. It would not have been lost on the earliest readers that this confession appears on the lips of a Roman centurion. As such, the confession would have carried a significance beyond those images of God's Son expressed within Second Temple Jewish texts.

At the halfway point of the narrative, Peter confesses that Jesus is the "Messiah" (8:29)—thus providing a pivot point in the story. That confession is followed in 8:31 by the first of three passion predictions (cf. also 9:31; 10:32–34) in which Jesus clarifies what it means for him to be the Messiah. From that point forward, the narrative moves in a different direction with greater emphasis on Jesus's impending death and resurrection. Then, at the climax of the Gospel when Jesus is hanging on the cross, a Roman centurion participating in the crucifixion confesses that he is the Son of God (15:39). The two titles applied to Jesus in 1:1 correspond to these two significant moments in the narrative—one at the midpoint and the other at the climax of the story. How are these observations significant for Mark's literary and theological rhetoric?

In these two moments, Peter and the centurion (1) represent Jewish and Roman perspectives, respectively, (2)

---

26. Kelly R. Iverson provides a compelling argument that this confession (1) represents a sincere confession, and (2) serves as an applause line within an ancient performative context; see "A Centurion's 'Confession': A Performance-Critical Analysis of Mark 15:39," *JBL* 130.2 (2011): 329–50.

represent insider and outsider perspectives, respectively, and (3) provide confessions that frame the entire narrative. Peter—a Jew and an intimate follower of Jesus—represents the *ultimate insider.* He has walked with Jesus. He has witnessed all of Jesus's exorcisms and deeds of power. He has been privy to the explanation of all of Jesus's parables. We should read his confession in the context of Jewish understandings of Messiah—even if his understanding of Jesus's messianic mission is incomplete and he is ultimately scolded by Jesus (8:31–33). Jesus is the Messiah. Peter gets at least that much correct.

In direct contrast with Peter, the centurion is a Roman soldier participating in the crucifixion of Jesus, and as such, he represents the *ultimate outsider.* He has not had contact with Jesus in the narrative prior to this moment. He has not heard Jesus preach publicly or explain the interpretation of his parables. Yet he confesses something of immense cosmic and theological significance at the climax of the Gospel story. We should read his confession in light of Roman understandings of the title son of God. Recognizing the contrast between the insights of the "insider" and "outsider" in this narrative frame is also critical for an appreciation of Mark's overall Christological presentation (see figure 4.1 below). The narrator identifies Jesus as the Messiah and Son of God (1:1). At the halfway point of the Gospel, a Jewish insider confesses that he is the Messiah. At the climax of the narrative a Roman outsider confesses that he is the Son of God. These perfectly placed confessions create a literary frame. Jesus has come to usher in God's kingdom and fulfill his mission—a mission that has significance for the entire world and is communicated in terms significant to both Jews and non-Jewish Romans.

FIGURE 4.1: MESSIAH AND SON OF GOD: A NARRATIVE FRAME

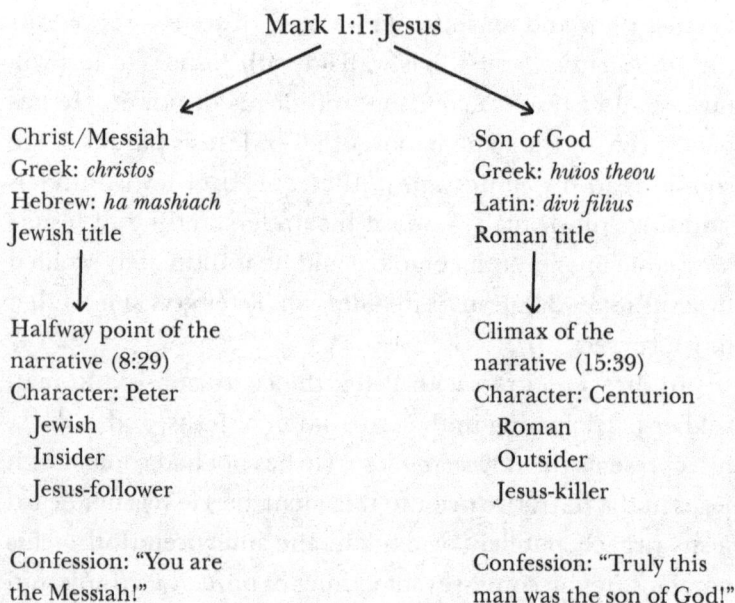

Mark 1:1: Jesus

Christ/Messiah
Greek: *christos*
Hebrew: *ha mashiach*
Jewish title

Son of God
Greek: *huios theou*
Latin: *divi filius*
Roman title

Halfway point of the
narrative (8:29)
Character: Peter
  Jewish
  Insider
  Jesus-follower

Climax of the
narrative (15:39)
Character: Centurion
  Roman
  Outsider
  Jesus-killer

Confession: "You are
the Messiah!"

Confession: "Truly this
man was the son of God!"

These two moments confirm what the audience
already knows while advancing their knowledge of
what these titles mean when applied to Jesus.

JESUS, THE "SON OF GOD"

As we conclude our examination of the theme of Jesus's identity in Mark, I close by reiterating the importance of wrestling with Jesus's status as "Son of God" to understand Mark's literary and theological agendas. Only by engaging the Gospel narrative can we progress from the knowledge *that* Jesus is the Son of God (1:1) to a fuller understanding of *how* he is the Son of God according to Mark. We have discovered that the Markan Son of God is the divinely commissioned (1:9–11) and sent representative of God (1:12–13; 12:1–12) who has been endowed with authority to teach (1:27–28; 9:7) and the power to overcome Satan and his emissaries (1:21–28; 5:1–20; 7:24–30; 9:14–29). The Son has also come to usher in the kingdom of God (1:14–15; on which see the next two chapters). We note further that the Son has a unique relationship to God as evidenced by two enigmatic "I am" texts (6:50; 14:62)—though we do not have space in this brief chapter to expand on this further.[27] We learn that the Son of God must be rejected and killed but will demonstrate the full consummation of his victory over Satan by rising from the dead (8:31; 9:31; 10:32–34; 12:1–12). Once Jesus has completed this work, he will occupy his rightful spot at God's right hand, and he will usher in the eschaton while coming with the clouds of heaven (14:62). Questions remain as to how we should understand Jesus in relation to early Christian claims about Jesus's humanity and divinity.[28] These questions ultimately lie outside the scope of the present chapter though they are important to a fuller understanding of Mark's Christology within early Christian doctrinal formulations. For now, the above summary represents a faithful understanding of the Markan Son of God that accounts for the worlds behind and within the text.

THE IDENTITY OF JESUS IN MARK

The past two chapters have focused on the complex theme of Jesus's identity in the Gospel of Mark. We have discovered

---

27. For reflections on this subject, Timothy Geddert, "The Implied YHWH Christology of Mark's Gospel: Mark's Challenge to the Reader to 'Connect the Dots,'" *BBR* 25.3 (2015): 325–40; and Christopher W. Skinner, "*Egō Eimi* in Mark and John: Exploring the Johannine Trajectory of a Received Memory of Jesus," *BR* 69 (forthcoming).

28. For differing perspectives on this important discussion, see the chapters on Mark in Simon Gathercole, *The Pre-Existent Son: Recovering the Christologies of the Synoptic Gospels* (Grand Rapids: Eerdmans, 2006); and J. R. Daniel Kirk, *A Man Attested by God: The Human Jesus of the Synoptic Gospels* (Grand Rapids: Eerdmans, 2016).

what it means for Jesus to be both the Messiah/Christ and Son of God. This twofold affirmation lies at the heart of everything that Mark wants to communicate to his audience in this narrative Christology. For Mark, Jesus is the fulfillment of long-held Jewish messianic expectations, even while he subverts and ultimately rejects some elements of those expectations in his ministry, death, and resurrection. But Jesus is also the royal and eschatological son of God who exists at the intersection of Jewish and Roman civil religion. As the royal son, Jesus is greater than David and he is greater than Caesar. He transcends the cultural and religious categories of both Jews and Romans and provides a new means of access to God. He is also the one authorized by the Father to usher in the kingdom of God on earth. We turn now to a consideration of that important theme.

FOR FURTHER READING

Carter, Warren. *Jesus and the Empire of God: Reading the Gospels in the Roman Empire*, Cascade Companions. Eugene, OR: Cascade, 2021.

Horsley, Richard A. *Hearing the Whole Story: The Politics of Plot in Mark's Gospel*. Louisville: Westminster John Knox, 2001.

Incigneri, Brian. *The Gospel to the Romans: The Setting and Rhetoric of Mark's Gospel*. BibInt 65. Leiden: Brill, 2003.

Peppard, Michael. *The Son of God in the Roman World: Divine Sonship in Its Social and Political Context*. Oxford: Oxford University Press, 2011.

Winn, Adam. *Reading Mark's Christology Under Caesar: Jesus the Messiah and Roman Imperial Ideology*. Downers Grove: IVP Academic, 2018.

Yarbro Collins, Adela. "Mark and His Readers: The Son of God Among Greeks and Romans." *HTR* 93.2 (2000): 85–100.

Yarbro Collins, Adela. "Mark and His Readers: The Son of God Among Jews." *HTR* 92.4 (1999): 393–408.

CHAPTER 5

The Kingdom of God in Mark (Part 1)

The Immediacy and Power of God's Reign

THE KINGDOM OF GOD IN MARKAN PERSPECTIVE

After the identity of Jesus, the kingdom of God is perhaps the key theme in Mark's Gospel. The character, shape, and arrival of the kingdom of God are all emphases in the teaching and ministry activities of the Markan Jesus. Modern readers of the NT regularly encounter important vocabulary that is informed by centuries of reflection and theological development. As discussed in the previous two chapters, the terms "Messiah" and "Son of God" are two such examples. While these terms have developed specific meanings within the various Christian theological traditions, they need to be placed in their appropriate historical, cultural, and religious contexts before we can understand how they are being used in the NT in general and the Gospel of Mark in particular. Another such example is the phrase "kingdom of God." Many contemporary readers regard this phrase as a substitute for "heaven," but that is not how it functions in the Gospel of Mark. For Mark, the kingdom of God (Greek: *basileia tou theou*) is a layered concept that is difficult to define by appealing to one specific idea.[1]

First, in Mark's economy, the kingdom is the inbreaking reign of God in the here and now that anticipates what will arrive decisively in the future (cf. 1:15; 9:1; 11:10; 15:43).[2] In a very real sense, the future has entered the present in the ministry of Jesus in a way that impacts the course of history. Consider the first occurrence of the phrase in Mark: "Now after John was arrested, Jesus came to Galilee, proclaiming the good news of God, and saying, 'The time is fulfilled, and the kingdom of God [*basileia tou theou*] has come near; repent, and believe in the good news'" (1:14–15). This is a narrative moment of critical importance. After being baptized by John (1:9–11) and tempted by Satan for forty days (1:12–13), Jesus returns victorious from the wilderness proclaiming that the reign of God has arrived. While not fully consummated, this kingdom has drawn near in a decisive way in Jesus's triumph over Satan in the wilderness. His announcement "implies that the prophecies of scripture and the hopes of the people are in the process of being fulfilled."[3]

To gain a better understanding of Mark's presentation of the kingdom, we must recognize that the Gospel depicts a cosmic battle between God and Satan that is already underway on earth. In the opening scenes of the Gospel, Jesus steps into that battle for the first time. The battle will

---

1. The term *basileia* appears twenty times in Mark, fifteen of which are direct references to the kingdom of God (1:15; 4:11, 26, 30; 6:23; 9:1, 47; 10:14, 15, 23, 24, 25; 12:34; 15:43).

2. Throughout this chapter and the next, I will use "kingdom," and "reign" interchangeably when referring to the Gospel's understanding of the kingdom of God.

3. Adela Yarbro Collins, *Mark: A Commentary*, Hermeneia (Minneapolis: Fortress, 2007), 154.

progress toward a climactic showdown in which Jesus—by the paradoxical means of death on a cross—prevails once and for all. While the wilderness temptations are only the beginning of Jesus's struggle in this cosmic battle, they nevertheless represent a real victory. Whereas the temptation and subsequent fall of Adam led to fear and anxiety within creation (cf. Gen 3:14–19), Jesus is described in this passage as being "with the wild beasts" (1:13), a phrase that reflects a state like Adam's peaceful relationship with all creation prior to the fall and the fulfillment of Israel's messianic hopes (see Isa 11:6–9). Jesus's wilderness experience thus constitutes a reversal of Adam's misfortunes and allows God's reign to "draw near," in a way that will permit the kingdom to increase slowly and incipiently, not unlike the growth of a mustard seed (cf. Mark 4:30–32). This tension between the embryonic inbreaking of God's reign on earth alongside the recognition that God's reign has not been fully consummated has often been referred to as "inaugurated eschatology," or more commonly by the phrase "already-not yet."[4] It is important to keep this tension in mind as we read the Gospel and reflect on Mark's specific presentation of the kingdom.

In addition to those texts that depict the kingdom as the inbreaking reign of God, we also encounter passages in Mark that refer to one *entering* the kingdom (9:47; 10:15, 23–25, 14:25). Against the backdrop of modern Christian theological ideas about the afterlife, this language has often been understood as referring to one's entrance into heaven.

---

4. Many Hellenistic Jewish and early Christian writings contain an eschatological dualism that contrasts the present evil age with the coming age in which God will right the world. This eschatological outlook has been labelled *futuristic eschatology*. Mark's *inaugurated eschatology* sees the reign of God entering this present evil age in and through the ministry of Jesus, though it has not yet been fully consummated.

However, such an understanding is anachronistic as the more developed doctrines of heaven and hell that attend contemporary Christian teaching did not emerge until much later.[5] It is better to understand these texts as referring not to a physical or spatial *realm* but to a *reality* into which those who are faithful to God will soon enter. Thus, for Mark, God's reign is an abiding reality that presents itself on earth in nascent forms in the ministry of Jesus, a reign that will be fully realized on earth as God rights the world once and for all in the approaching eschaton.

With this understanding in mind, we can observe the kingdom of God emerging in different ways throughout the Gospel of Mark. At certain turns, God's reign bursts into the world decisively with immediacy and power. At others, God's reign is shrouded in both mystery and secrecy, and surfaces in the most unexpected ways. We will discuss this latter phenomenon at length in the next chapter. Our guiding observation in this chapter and the next is that the kingdom of God in Mark's Gospel is multifaceted and unpredictable. Therefore, we must pay careful attention to the various contours of Mark's presentation of the kingdom to gain a better understanding of Jesus's ministry in the Gospel as well as the mysterious nature of God's presence in a world that is under siege from satanic forces. In the remainder of this chapter and the one that follows, we will examine Mark's emphasis on the immediacy and power of God's kingdom alongside its secretive and mysterious emergence in the world.

---

5. In her monograph, *Educating Early Christians Through the Rhetoric of Hell: 'Weeping and Gnashing of Teeth' as Paideia in Matthew and the Early Church*, WUNT 2.382 (Tübingen: Mohr Siebeck, 2014), Meghan Henning makes a compelling argument that early Christian views of hell developed—beginning with the Gospel of Matthew—as a distinctive approach to religious instruction.

MARK'S LITERARY STYLE AND THE KINGDOM OF GOD

To appreciate Mark's narrative world—and specifically his presentation of the kingdom of God within that world—we must familiarize ourselves with the ways in which he communicates. This necessitates an awareness of the rhetoric of the narrative (Mark's storytelling) and the means by which he communicates this rhetoric (Mark's grammar and syntax). We begin here with a consideration of the latter.

The Gospel of Mark is known for its rough style of Greek prose. Scholars have long recognized that Mark's prose lacks the elegance and sophistication of other NT texts like the Gospel of Luke, Hebrews, and 1 Peter—all of which are much more stylized. By contrast, Mark's prose is simplistic and artless, particularly in his use of Greek prepositions.[6] Nearly 65 percent of the sentences in Mark's Gospel begin with the word "and" (Greek: *kai*), a feature that contributes to a style of writing known as *parataxis*. A paratactic style is characterized by placing short phrases together without the use of subordinating conjunctions. Well-known examples of parataxis include Julius Caesar's famous declaration, "I came, I saw, I conquered," and the classic M&M's advertising slogan, "Melts in your mouth, not in your hands." Mark's use of parataxis creates a fast-paced narrative that jumps

---

6. When we compare how both Matthew and Luke make use of Mark's Gospel, one interesting observation is that both regularly change his Greek prepositions and often in the same texts. Hellenistic Greek had nearly two dozen prepositions from which to choose. By contrast, Hebrew and Aramaic had only four primary prepositions, each of which was used to express a range of ideas. Mark's limited use of prepositions is further evidence to support the observation that there is significant bilingual interference throughout the Gospel.

quickly from action to action and scene to scene. This style
is also aided by the use of phrases like *kai egeneto* ("and it happened"), which serves primarily to advance the action of the
narrative.[7] Another phrase, *kai euthys* ("and immediately"), is
a virtually inescapable feature of Mark's literary style. Overall,
the term *euthys* appears forty-one times across the Gospel and
in all but three chapters, and the specific phrase *kai euthys*
appears twenty-five of those times.[8] Those accustomed to
reading the Gospel only in English may find it difficult to
get a sense of the rapidity with which this term occurs since
some translations interchange "immediately" with phrases
like "and then," "just then," "at once," "at this," "forthwith,"
or "straightaway."[9] It is safe to say that this particular term
is meaningful for Mark, though there is debate as to what
it signals. It should come as no surprise that grammarians
and commentators have reflected a great deal on Mark's use
of this term, and their conclusions are often predictably at
cross-purposes.

Specialists in Greek grammar have sometimes regarded
the phrase *kai euthys* as a remnant of Mark's lived experience
as a Jewish speaker of Aramaic attempting to communicate in

---

7. Cf. 1:9; 2:23; 4:4, 10; 9:7 (twice), 26; 11:19. In the Septuagint, the phrase
kai egeneto often translates the Hebrew *wayyehi*, which is more properly a narrative
marker and is not necessarily supposed to be translated. Mark appears to have
inherited this storytelling convention from those who translated the Hebrew
Scriptures into Greek.

8. The term *euthys* appears in the following verses: 1:10, 12, 18, 20, 21, 23,
28, 29, 30, 42, 43; 2:8, 12; 3:6; 4:5, 15, 16, 17, 29; 5:2, 29, 30, 42; 6:25, 27, 45, 50,
54; 7:25; 8:10; 9:15, 20, 24; 10:52; 11:2, 3; 14:43, 45, 72; 15:1. The variant spelling
eutheōs appears in 7:35. The expression is used in Mark more than all other NT
texts combined.

9. Contemporary English translations that consistently render *euthys* as
"immediately" include the ESV and the NASB. For those who do not read Greek,
it may be helpful to consult one of these translations when attempting to trace
this phrase throughout the Gospel.

Greek.[10] Anyone who has learned another language is aware that there is no such thing as a one-to-one correspondence between one thought world and another. A common experience for those navigating a new language is thinking in one's first language while attempting to translate effectively into the second. This experience often generates a linguistic hybrid in which elements of both languages are present—a phenomenon known as bilingual interference. In the specific case of Mark's Gospel, we refer to this phenomenon as Semitic interference, since various elements of Aramaic and Hebrew appear to be present in Mark's Greek. Because the consistent use of *kai euthys* creates an awkward syntax, some have been quick to dismiss the phrase as an anomalous feature of Mark's prose that has no particular significance at the level of the narrative. I have even encountered scholars who argue that the phrase should be read as a vocalized pause, similar to the use of "uh" or "um" by speakers of English. While observations about Mark's awkward syntax are valid and deserving of serious attention, they should not be the final word on the subject. It is important to remember that multiple things can be true at the same time, a necessary reminder when we are seeking to disentangle some of the thorny issues in biblical interpretation. In other words, we

---

10. On this, Paul Ellingworth notes that "the problem is not just a problem of style: it is also a problem of meaning. *Euthus* [sic] in Mark often does not mean 'immediately.' Indeed, it may not even be an expression of time at all. Perhaps in the Aramaic sources on which most of Mark's gospel is based, the word was the same one that other gospels translate as 'behold!' or 'look!' It is probably no accident that Mark almost always uses *euthus* [sic] in narrative and 'behold!' in words spoken by someone in the gospel story" ("How Soon is 'Immediately' in Mark?" *Bible Translator* 29 [1978]: 414–19 [here 414]). For more on the peculiar features of Mark's Greek, see Rodney J. Decker, "Markan Idiolect in the Study of the Greek New Testament" in *The Language of the New Testament: Context, History, Development*, ed. Stanley E. Porter and Andrew W. Pitts, ECHC 3 (Leiden: Brill, 2013), 43–66; and W. S. Vorster, "Bilingualism and the Greek of the New Testament: Semitic Interference in the Gospel of Mark," *Neot* 24.2 (1990): 215–28.

can rightly regard the consistent use of *kai euthys* as awkward at the level of Greek syntax and still acknowledge that it is an important element of Mark's storytelling technique.

In many instances, Mark's use of "immediately" attests to the reign of God breaking into the world with immediacy and power, and in these instances—often in the context of healing miracles and exorcisms—Mark's use of *kai euthys* is a critical part of his presentation of the kingdom of God. In other instances, *euthys* either works at the discursive level and simply contributes to the pace of the narrative and the rapid shifting from scene to scene or relates to the urgency of the story. Let us consider the following five examples.

1. Jesus Is Baptized (Mark 1:9–11)

In those days Jesus came from Nazareth of Galilee and was baptized by John in the Jordan. And *just as* [*kai euthys*] he was coming up out of the water, he saw the heavens torn apart and the Spirit descending like a dove on him. And a voice came from heaven, "You are my Son, the Beloved; with you I am well pleased." (emphasis added)

Here we have our first occurrence of the phrase *kai euthys* in the Gospel of Mark, and there are few examples that better exemplify its use to signal the inbreaking reign of God in the world. As Jesus is baptized—which is ostensibly the moment that prepares him for his public vocation—he *immediately* sees the skies torn apart and simultaneously experiences both the voice of God and the descent of the Spirit. This passage prepares the audience for the next scene where Jesus is *immediately* driven by the Spirit into the wilderness to be tested by Satan (1:12), followed by the initial groups of disciples abandoning their nets to follow Jesus *immediately*

(1:18, 20), and further followed by the *immediate* healing of a leper who comes to Jesus for help (1:42). The phrase *kai euthys* occurs at critical moments throughout Mark's first chapter and its literary and theological significance are signaled by its appearance in this foundational passage in 1:9–11. These initial scenes will prepare the audience for the immediate emergence of God's kingdom and its urgency in various ways throughout the remainder of the Gospel.

2. Jesus Heals a Paralytic (Mark 2:1–12)

When he returned to Capernaum after some days, it was reported that he was at home. So many gathered around that there was no longer room for them, not even in front of the door, and he was speaking the word to them. Then some people came, bringing to him a paralyzed man, carried by four of them. And when they could not bring him to Jesus because of the crowd, they removed the roof above him, and after having dug through it, they let down the mat on which the paralytic lay. When Jesus saw their faith, he said to the paralytic, "Son, your sins are forgiven." Now some of the scribes were sitting there questioning in their hearts, "Why does this fellow speak in this way? It is blasphemy! Who can forgive sins but God alone?" <u>At once</u> [*kai euthys*] Jesus perceived in his spirit that they were discussing these questions among themselves, and he said to them, "Why do you raise such questions in your hearts? Which is easier: to say to the paralytic, 'Your sins are forgiven,' or to say, 'Stand up and take your mat and walk'? But so that you may know that the Son of Man has authority on earth to forgive sins"—he said to the paralytic—"I say to you, stand up, take your mat, and go to your

home." And he stood up _and immediately_ [*kai euthys*]
took the mat and went out before all of them; so that
they were all amazed and glorified God, saying, "We
have never seen anything like this!" (emphasis added)

This is the first of several examples we will consider
here of Jesus healing an individual in a brief and decisive
moment. Twice in this passage Mark uses the phrase *kai
euthys* to depict the inbreaking of the kingdom. A group of
individuals brings a paralytic to Jesus with hopes that he can
heal him. After Jesus announces to the paralytic that his sins
are forgiven, some religious leaders who are present object
to this language. Jesus is *immediately* aware that he is being
criticized (2:8), but not because he has heard the criticisms
directly. Rather, to use Mark's language, he perceives this
"in his spirit." Perhaps a better way to think of this is that
these criticisms have been revealed to him by God. Then, in
a climactic moment in which Jesus addresses the religious
leaders on one side and the paralytic on the other, he commands the paralytic to take up his mat and walk, which he
proceeds to do *immediately* (2:11–12). It is also important for us
to recognize here that Jesus is able to accomplish this healing
merely with a word. The ability to heal simply by speaking
makes Jesus uncommon among the healers known to us from
the ancient Jewish and Greco-Roman worlds.[11] This display of

---

11. Numerous healers, miracle workers, and magicians appear in various
Greco-Roman and Jewish texts from around the time of Jesus. These include
healers associated with the cult of Asclepius and Jewish figures such as Honi the
Circle Drawer, Eleazar, and Hanina ben Dosa, among others. Often, healings
and exorcisms are accompanied by elaborate rituals, incantations, and the use of
physical objects. The ability to heal sickness and cast out unclean spirits simply
by speaking makes Jesus uncommon among the ancient healers about whom
we have any substantive information. One possible counterexample would be
Greek Magical Papyri, which feature magical spells, hymns, and other ritualistic
speech.

Jesus's authority over disease, disorder, and eventually death (see the discussion of 5:35–43 below) is the first of numerous such examples of the reign of God breaking into the world with both immediacy and power.

3. Jesus Heals a Hemorrhaging Woman (Mark 5:25–34)

Now there was a woman who had been suffering from hemorrhages for twelve years. She had endured much under many physicians, and had spent all that she had; and she was no better, but rather grew worse. She had heard about Jesus, and came up behind him in the crowd and touched his cloak, for she said, "If I but touch his clothes, I will be made well." *Immediately* [*kai euthys*] her hemorrhage stopped; and she felt in her body that she was healed of her disease. *Immediately* [*kai euthys*] aware that power had gone forth from him, Jesus turned about in the crowd and said, "Who touched my clothes?" And his disciples said to him, "You see the crowd pressing in on you; how can you say, 'Who touched me?'" He looked all around to see who had done it. But the woman, knowing what had happened to her, came in fear and trembling, fell down before him, and told him the whole truth. He said to her, "Daughter, your faith has made you well; go in peace, and be healed of your disease." (emphasis added)

As in the healing passage we just considered (2:1–12), there are again two instances of the phrase *kai euthys* in this text, both of which relate to the emergence of the kingdom. The first reference points to the healing of a physical malady that had persisted for twelve years. With one touch, the woman is *immediately* healed (5:29). It should be noted

that unlike other instances of healing in Mark, the physical
contact leading to this restoration is not initiated by Jesus
but rather by the ailing woman. Even in a passive state,
Mark's Jesus is an effective conduit for the emergence of the
kingdom; he has unparalleled dominion over the forces of
death.[12] As with the story of the paralytic considered above,
the second use of *kai euthys* alludes to Jesus's cognition at a
supernatural level. He is *immediately* aware that power has
gone forth from him (5:30); again, we should regard this
awareness as a revelation from God. Once again, in light
of the developing narrative rhetoric, it is difficult to regard
these uses of *kai euthys* as something other than deliberate
attempts to depict the immediacy and power of God's reign
breaking into the world.

4. Jesus Heals the Daughter of Jairus (Mark 5:35–43)

While he was still speaking, some people came from
the leader's house to say, "Your daughter is dead. Why
trouble the teacher any further?" But overhearing
what they said, Jesus said to the leader of the synagogue, "Do not fear, only believe." He allowed no
one to follow him except Peter, James, and John, the
brother of James. When they came to the house of the
leader of the synagogue, he saw a commotion, people
weeping and wailing loudly. When he had entered,
he said to them, "Why do you make a commotion
and weep? The child is not dead but sleeping." And
they laughed at him. Then he put them all outside,
and took the child's father and mother and those who
were with him, and went in where the child was. He

---

12. See the excellent treatment of this in Matthew Thiessen, *Jesus and the
Forces of Death: The Gospels' Portrayal of Ritual Impurity Within First-Century Judaism*
(Grand Rapids: Baker Academic, 2021).

took her by the hand and said to her, "*Talitha cum*," which means, "Little girl, get up!" <u>*And immediately*</u> [*kai euthys*] the girl got up and began to walk about (she was twelve years of age). At this they were overcome with amazement. He strictly ordered them that no one should know this, and told them to give her something to eat. (emphasis added)

This story of Jairus's daughter being raised from the dead is intimately connected to our previous passage in which the hemorrhaging woman is healed. Together, the stories of these two women constitute an intercalated passage, or "sandwich," that is meant to draw connections between the experiences of both. (For more on this uniquely Markan literary technique, see figure 5.1.) Within the broader context of the intercalated unit 5:21–43, Jesus is in the midst of a crowd when he is first approached by a synagogue official named Jairus with a request to heal his dying daughter (5:21–24). After the story concludes its focus on the healing of the hemorrhaging woman (5:25–34), the narrative returns to Jairus, who learns that his daughter has died. Exhorting him to believe, Jesus travels home with Jairus for the purposes of resurrecting the girl. Again, with a touch, this time accompanied by a command that Mark recounts in Aramaic ("*Talitha koum*") along with a translation ("Little girl, get up!"), the girl's life is *immediately* restored (5:42). The proof of this genuine resurrection is that the little girl instantly gets up and begins walking about, to the astonishment of those who are present. There can hardly be a more powerful display of God's reign bursting forth into the world than the restoration of a human life from the dead as a demonstration of God's dominion over the power of death itself.

5. Bartimaeus Receives His Sight (Mark 10:46–52)

They came to Jericho. As he and his disciples and
a large crowd were leaving Jericho, Bartimaeus son
of Timaeus, a blind beggar, was sitting by the road-
side. When he heard that it was Jesus of Nazareth, he
began to shout out and say, "Jesus, Son of David, have
mercy on me!"

Many sternly ordered him to be quiet, but he
cried out even more loudly, "Son of David, have mercy
on me!" Jesus stood still and said, "Call him here."
And they called the blind man, saying to him, "Take
heart; get up, he is calling you." So throwing off his
cloak, he sprang up and came to Jesus. Then Jesus
said to him, "What do you want me to do for you?"
The blind man said to him, "My teacher, let me see
again." Jesus said to him, "Go; your faith has made
you well." _Immediately_ [_kai euthys_] he regained his sight
and followed him on the way. (emphasis added)

As in the healing passages we have already considered,
blind Bartimaeus approaches Jesus, despite the protestations
of others, and begs for mercy (10:47–48). A brief conversation clarifies the type of "mercy" he seeks—he wants to have
his vision restored (10:51). As in 2:11, Jesus issues a simple
verbal command that leads to the _immediate_ restoration of
Bartimaeus's sight (10:52). At this, Bartimaeus begins to follow Jesus, which provides an ironic twist to the story's end.
Jesus's command for him to "go" carries the sense of "depart
from here" but his restoration leads him to begin following
Jesus "on the way" (Greek: _en tē hodō_)—a phrase associated
with discipleship in Mark.[13]

---

13. Mark's understanding of discipleship will be treated in chapter 7.

FIGURE 5.1

Markan "Sandwiches": Intercalations in Mark

In these constructions, the narrator begins a story that is interrupted by a second story. Once the second story has been completed, the narrator returns to the first story and brings it to completion. Thus, one story appears to have been "sandwiched" between the two halves of another. The two stories usually contain different characters, focalize in different locations, and are characterized by dramatic irony. Mark also draws a connection between the two groups of characters. Units generally treated as sandwiches include:

- 3:21–35: Jesus's family insists he is out of his mind while the Jewish leaders insist that he is demon-possessed. Rejecting both groups, Jesus establishes a "new family."
- 5:21–43: Physical contact with Jesus heals two women. Contact with the deceased daughter of Jairus and the hemorrhaging woman should render Jesus unclean. Instead, both women are restored.
- 6:6b–30: Mission and martyrdom: the sending of the Twelve is tied to the death of John the Baptist at Herod's hand.
- 11:12–25: An enacted parable: Jesus curses the fig tree for its literal fruitlessness then curses the temple for its spiritual fruitlessness.
- 14:1–11: An insider (Judas) plots to kill Jesus while

> an outsider (the woman of Bethany) anoints Jesus
> in preparation for his burial.
> - 14:53–72: Peter is "outside" denying Jesus while
>   Jesus is "inside" being questioned by the Sanhedrin.
>   Jesus confesses the truth while Peter denies it.

We have not considered every occurrence of the phrase *kai euthys* in the Gospel, as our discussion is intentionally limited in the interests of space. However, if the foregoing examination has revealed anything, it is that when we encounter the term "immediately" in the Gospel of Mark we must approach with care and read with nuance. There are times when the term simply contributes to the rapid pace of the narrative. In other instances, it helps paint a vivid picture of the circumstances surrounding Jesus's battle with satanic forces.[14] However, as we have also seen, those circumstances are met and matched by Jesus's response, which instantly ushers in a powerful manifestation of God's presence here on earth. In the above texts we have observed God's kingdom arriving decisively and urgently each time in a context in which the phrase *kai euthys* appears. Careful attention to this recurring phrase and the themes it evokes can teach us a great deal about Mark's vision of the kingdom of God.

JESUS, EXORCISM, AND THE REIGN OF GOD

When we return to the battle between God and Satan that provides the cosmological framework for the Gospel, we find

---

14. See, e.g., 1:23; 6:27; 14:43, 72; 15:1.

that another critical component of Mark's presentation of the immediacy and power of the kingdom is Jesus's role as an exorcist. One of the most important and distinctive elements of Jesus's vocation in Mark is his practice of casting out unclean spirits. Exorcisms play such a foundational role in Jesus's public ministry that when he appoints the twelve disciples, they are commissioned for three specific things, one of which is to cast out demons (see 3:14–15).

As mentioned above, Jesus's initial victory over Satan in the wilderness constitutes a reversal of Adam's misfortunes in the garden. His preaching of the kingdom begins in earnest after this reversal is narrated (cf. 1:14–15), and his ministry is characterized by actions that depict an ongoing battle with the forces of Satan. This battle is most clearly seen in the casting out of unclean spirits, which Graham Twelftree has helpfully characterized as "power-encounters" between God and Satan.[15] These moments of direct contact between Jesus and satanic emissaries represent another manifestation of the kingdom of God with both immediacy and power. On this, Twelftree notes, "Uniquely, Jesus appears to have taken his exorcisms not as signs or evidence of the *expected Kingdom of God but, along with other healings, as its realization.*"[16] Against this backdrop, we should not overlook the subtle connection between John's announcement of the coming of "the stronger one" (Greek: *ho ischyroteros*; 1:7), Jesus's triumph over Satan during his period of testing (1:12–13), and his later parabolic discussion of binding the "strong one" (Greek: *ho ischyros*) before plundering his house (3:22–27). Throughout the

---

15. Graham Twelftree, *In the Name of Jesus: Exorcism Among Early Christians* (Grand Rapids: Baker Academic, 2007), 46.

16. Graham Twelftree, "Exorcism," *Oxford Bibliographies*, March 21, 2024, https://www.oxfordbibliographies.com/display/document/obo-9780195393361 /obo-9780195393361-0272.xml (emphasis added).

Gospel Satan represents "the strong one," but Jesus will prove over and over again in their encounters to be "the stronger one"—a scenario resulting from Jesus's initial victory in the wilderness.

It seems clear that the kingdom of God as envisioned by Mark is at least partially concerned with purity. This is likely one reason he uses the terms "demon" and "unclean spirit" synonymously throughout the Gospel.[17] In other words, the Markan Jesus has a problem with impurity, and in order to be a conduit for ushering in the kingdom, he must establish purity where impurity presently exists, which is a proleptic projection of the kingdom's absolute purity in the eschaton.[18] Sometimes Jesus accomplishes this by healing an infirmity or disease, as we saw in several of the passages considered in the previous section. Jesus routinely accomplishes this by casting out the source of impurity, and this is where his role as an exorcist becomes critical to Mark's presentation of the kingdom.[19] With one possible but debated exception, there appear to be no exorcisms in the Hebrew Bible.[20] Therefore,

---

17. The terms "demon" (Greek: *daimonion*) and "unclean spirit" (Greek: *pneuma akatharton*) are used interchangeably by Mark. "Demon" and its verbal cognate are used fifteen times in Mark (1:32, 34 [twice], 39; 3:15, 22 [twice]; 5:15, 16, 18; 6:13; 7:26, 29, 30; 9:38), while "unclean spirit" appears eleven times (1:23, 26, 27; 3:11, 30; 5:2, 8, 13; 6:7; 7:25; 9:25).

18. A prolepsis is a way of looking forward in anticipation of an event while speaking of that event as if it has already taken place. When I use the terms "proleptic" and "prolepsis" here, I am referring to the fully realized reign of God on earth.

19. Purity was an important idea in ancient Judaism. On the distinction between moral impurity, which is generated by sin, and ritual impurity, which is generated by various bodily functions, see Jonathan Klawans, *Impurity and Sin in Ancient Judaism* (Oxford: Oxford University Press, 2000). On the idea of Jesus recognizing and removing the sources of ritual impurity rather than opposing purity laws within Judaism, see Thiessen, *Jesus and the Forces of Death*.

20. Some regard the story of the harp-playing David soothing Saul—who is tormented by an evil spirit—as a type of exorcism; see 1 Sam 16:14–23.

it is worth pausing our discussion to consider when this practice developed within Judaism. This will help us better understand Mark's presentation of Jesus as an exorcist.

The practice of exorcism is attested in texts from Mesopotamia and throughout the ancient Near East. It can best be defined as seeking to cast out a demonic force or personified sickness through a ritual or incantation in the name of a deity that both the exorcist and afflicted recognize as authoritative. The first explicit references to exorcism in any Jewish text are in Tobit 3:8, 6:7–9, and 8:1–3 (ca. 3rd cent.–2nd cent. BCE). Those texts picture what could be described as an informal exorcism, where a woman named Sarah has been possessed by a demon named Asmodeus. Sarah's husband, Tobias, is instructed to place a fish liver and heart atop glowing embers to repulse the demon with the resulting aroma. Josephus (ca. 93–94 CE) also recounts a healer named Eleazar attempting to cast out demons by drawing them out through the nostrils (*Antiquities of the Jews* 8.42–49). In addition to these texts, we also have several references to exorcism in the Dead Sea Scrolls (ca. 3rd cent. BCE–1st cent. CE).[21]

By the time of Jesus, the practice of exorcism was accepted within various expressions of Judaism. However, as an exorcist, the Markan Jesus appears to be distinctive in a number of respects. First, unlike other Jewish practitioners, Jesus does not use incantations, songs, or physical implements. In most instances, he simply uses a verbal command (though see his use of spittle in 7:31–37; 8:22–26). Second, with the exception of the healing in 8:22–26, the encounters between

---

21. Four psalms found in the Dead Sea Scrolls refer to exorcism, one of which is Psalm 91. The other three fragmentary texts—one attributed to Solomon and two attributed to David—were otherwise unknown before their discovery.

Jesus and the demonic or Jesus and the infirm all appear to be instantaneous and on the spot.[22] Unlike other instances from Jewish literature, no advanced planning goes into the event. Third, and most importantly for our present discussion, in each case, after Jesus's intervention, the wicked spirit departs immediately and without further incident.

In Mark, Jesus's role as an exorcist is mentioned in passing twice (1:32–34; 3:20–28) and depicted in detail four different times (1:21–28; 5:1–20; 7:24–30; 9:14–29). Three of these longer exorcism stories follow a fairly predictable pattern: (1) there is a confrontation between Jesus and a demoniac accompanied by an acclamation or request, either from the demoniac or someone associated with it, (2) this is followed by a command from Jesus that results in the expulsion of the unclean spirit, and (3) the story ends with a report of the responses of those witnessing the event. For more on this, see the chart on the following page.

In each of the stories recounted here, Jesus easily overcomes the unclean spirit and vanquishes it immediately with a word of power. As before, we witness the decisive inbreaking of God's reign in these various power-encounters.

The only remaining example of an exorcism we have yet to consider appears in Mark 7:24–30 and departs from the above pattern. Here, Jesus is approached by a Syrophoenician woman who, like Jairus in 5:21–43, has come to advocate for an ailing daughter:

---

22. A lot of ink has been spilled over Jesus's seeming inability to heal the blind man completely the first time. Within the context of a narrative approach to the text, it is probably best to connect this two-stage healing to the spiritual blindness of the disciples who understand that Jesus is the Messiah but cannot square that with the message of his suffering and death in the very next pericope. On this, see Francis J. Moloney, *The Gospel of Mark: A Commentary* (Peabody, MA: Hendrickson, 2002), 162–64.

FIGURE 5.2: EXORCISM STORIES IN MARK

Text	Confrontation/ Request	Command/ Expulsion	Responses of Witnesses
1:21–28	There was in their synagogue a man with an unclean spirit. (1:23) "What have you to do with us, Jesus of Nazareth? Have you come to destroy us? I know who you are, the Holy One of God." (1:24)	"Be silent, and come out of him!" (1:25) And the unclean spirit, convulsing him and crying with a loud voice, came out of him. (1:26)	"What is this? A new teaching—with authority! He commands even the unclean spirits, and they obey him." (1:27)
5:1–20	And when he had stepped out of the boat, immediately a man from the tombs with an unclean spirit met him. . . . When he saw Jesus from a distance, he ran and bowed down before him. (5:2–6) He shouted at the top of his voice, "What have you to do with me, Jesus, Son of the Most High God? I adjure you by God, do not torment me." (5:7)	For he had said to him, "Come out of the man, you unclean spirit!" Then Jesus asked him, "What is your name?" He replied, "My name is Legion, for we are many." (5:8–9) And the unclean spirits came out and entered the swine, and the herd . . . stampeded down the steep bank into the sea and were drowned in the sea. (5:13)	Those who had seen what had happened to the man possessed by demons and to the swine reported it. Then they began to beg Jesus to leave their neighborhood. (5:16–17)
9:14–29	When the spirit saw him, immediately it convulsed the boy, and he fell on the ground and rolled about, foaming at the mouth. (9:20)	"You spirit that keeps this boy from speaking and hearing, I command you, come out of him, and never enter him again!" (9:25) After crying out and convulsing him terribly, it came out, and the boy was like a corpse. (9:26)	Most of them said, "He is dead." (9:26) When he had entered the house, his disciples asked him privately, "Why could we not cast it out?" (9:28)

> From there he set out and went away to the region of Tyre.
> He entered a house and did not want anyone to know he
> was there. Yet he could not escape notice, but a woman
> whose little daughter had an unclean spirit immediately
> heard about him, and she came and bowed down at his
> feet. Now the woman was a Gentile, of Syrophoenician
> origin. She begged him to cast the demon out of her
> daughter. He said to her, "Let the children be fed first,
> for it is not fair to take the children's food and throw it
> to the dogs." But she answered him, "Sir, even the dogs
> under the table eat the children's crumbs." Then he said
> to her, "For saying that, you may go—the demon has left
> your daughter." So she went home, found the child lying
> on the bed, and the demon gone. (7:24–30)

This passage departs from the pattern we have seen in other
healings and exorcisms to this point in that Jesus has no direct
contact with the afflicted individual. He does not touch, nor
does he speak directly to the daughter of the Syrophoenician
woman. In fact, he never even meets her! This story is unique
in a couple of respects.

First, in seeking to dismiss the woman, Jesus utters a
mini-parable about food, children, and dogs. But the woman
responds by boldly entering the world of that parable with an
uncompromising retort that reiterates her petition. We do not
regularly witness this sort of interaction between Jesus and
others in Mark's Gospel. This response appears to surprise
Jesus, and it moves him to acknowledge the woman's faith and
grant her petition (7:29–30).

Second, the audience learns something new about Jesus's
ability as an exorcist from this passage. It is not necessary for
Jesus to touch or even speak directly to the demoniac for the
exorcism to be effective. As in the healing stories in 2:1–12

and 10:46–52, Jesus is able to accomplish this exorcism with only a word. But unlike those stories, this exorcism is distinctive in that it takes place from a distance, and it happens instantaneously. Here we have yet one more example of the reign of God emerging with immediacy and power.

Jesus's regular practice of casting out unclean spirits is an important element of Mark's overall presentation of the kingdom. In addition to exorcising demons, Jesus is able to offer consolation, healing, restoration, and even new life. That he can accomplish all of this through a variety of means—a simple word, a touch, an up-close interaction, or a long-distance intervention—is further evidence of his distinctiveness and is instructive for our developing vision of God's reign in the Gospel of Mark.

THE TRANSFIGURATION AS THE KINGDOM COMING WITH POWER

Before concluding this chapter, we must briefly consider one more example of God's reign appearing with power. This text, while often misunderstood throughout the history of interpretation, has the potential to contribute significantly to our understanding of the kingdom in Mark. In 8:34–38, as Jesus is instructing both his disciples and a larger crowd about the costs of discipleship, he proclaims, "Those who are ashamed of me and of my words in this adulterous and sinful generation, of them the Son of Man will also be ashamed when he comes in the glory of his Father with the holy angels" (8:38). While the chapter ends here, commentators widely acknowledge that the first verse of the next chapter serves as the conclusion to this mini discourse. There Jesus proclaims, "Truly I tell you, there are some standing here who will not taste death until they see that the kingdom of God has come

with power" (9:1). This one proclamation has a long and
complicated history of interpretation that has often failed
to take into account both the developing narrative rhetoric
and where this particular pronouncement is situated in the
Gospel story.

A previous generation of scholarship attempted to use
Jesus's pronouncement in 9:1 as a basis for insisting that
the historical Jesus earnestly believed that the kingdom of
God would be fully realized on earth during his lifetime.[23]
Regardless of whether the historical Jesus held such a view—
and we have no way of knowing with any certainty—we must
recognize that such an argument misses the point of what
is happening *at this particular point in the text.* This is a good
place to pause briefly and remind ourselves that extracting
a singular text out of a broader narrative to make a specific
historical argument can raise unnecessary complications.
While we want to take into account all historical information
that will allow us to better understand the text and the world
behind it, it is clear that Mark has a distinctive presentation
of Jesus's life and ministry that often differs from other narrative portraits. Thus, it makes better sense to approach such
difficult passages by trying to understand first how they are
functioning in their immediate and proximate contexts *within
the narrative itself.* Against that backdrop, when we consider
the pronouncement in 9:1 in this way, it is not difficult to
conclude that it is intimately connected to, and in fact anticipates what comes after it—the story of Jesus's transfiguration.
We read:

---

23. Decades of scholarly reflection on this one saying have focused on a
handful of questions including (1) whether or not this saying goes back to the
historical Jesus, (2) whether or not the saying refers to the *parousia* (second coming) or possibly the *eschaton* or resurrection, and (3) how to understand Jesus's
own view of the end of the world in light of the fact that he made such a promise
that went unfulfilled.

Six days later, Jesus took with him Peter and James and
John, and led them up a high mountain apart, by themselves. And he was transfigured before them, and his
clothes became dazzling white, such as no one on earth
could bleach them. And there appeared to them Elijah
with Moses, who were talking with Jesus. Then Peter said to
Jesus, "Rabbi, it is good for us to be here; let us make three
dwellings, one for you, one for Moses, and one for Elijah."
He did not know what to say, for they were terrified. Then
a cloud overshadowed them, and from the cloud there
came a voice, "This is my Son, the Beloved; listen to him!"
Suddenly when they looked around, they saw no one with
them any more, but only Jesus. (9:2–8)

Let us briefly return to the immediate context of this pericope. In 9:1, Jesus proclaims that *some who are standing in his
presence will not die before they see the kingdom coming in power.*
Then, six days later he takes three of his disciples (that is, *some
of those who are standing in his presence in 9:1*) up onto a high
mountain, away from everyone else. These three disciples are
privileged to experience multiple phenomena that we should
rightly regard as manifestations of the kingdom coming with
power—the very thing Jesus predicted at the end of the previous unit.

First, the three disciples see Jesus completely transfigured before them. The Greek word often rendered "transfigured" or "transformed" is the word from which we get
our English term, "metamorphosis." Here Jesus undergoes a
transformation in which his clothes become dazzlingly white
beyond earthly abilities to brighten them. It is clear from
Peter's confused response in 9:5 that the disciples do not
have the categories to understand or explain what they are
experiencing.

Second, the disciples also see two figures of major importance to the religious life of Israel: Elijah and Moses. Some
have argued that Elijah and Moses represent the Law and the
Prophets, and that may well be the case, though one would
typically expect Moses to be mentioned first if that construction were in view here. Inasmuch as Moses and Elijah each
experienced theophanies on a mountain (cf. Exod 19:16–25;
1 Kgs 19:11–18), it seems likely that their presence in this text
is confirming this as a moment of theophany for Peter, James,
and John. Their experience of God's otherworldly presence
in this world is intended as part and parcel of the inbreaking
of the kingdom.

Third, and perhaps most significantly, a cloud descends,
and the disciples hear the very voice of God. This cloud is
most likely intended to evoke visions of the exodus when a
pillar of cloud led the wandering Israelites by day (cf. Exod
13:21–22; 14:19, 24; 33:9–10). Thus, the cloud is further representative of God's presence, offering more evidence that this
entire episode is intended as a theophany, and confirming
our understanding of this event as an example of the coming
of the kingdom with power. This is the second time the narrative audience has heard the voice of God, but it is the first
time anyone in the narrative other than Jesus has heard this
voice. The first time God spoke was during Jesus's baptism
in 1:11: "_You_ [sing.] are my Son, whom I love; with _you_ [sing.]
I am well pleased" (emphasis added). Notice that the voice
of God addresses Jesus directly in this text, but there is no
indication that others hear what is being said. When God
speaks for a second time in 9:7, however, he addresses the
disciples directly, "_This_ is my son, whom I love. [You, plural]
Listen to him!" (NIV; emphasis added).

While the specific phrase "kingdom of God" is not used

in 9:2–8, it should not be ignored that in this enigmatic scene, Peter, James, and John witness the inbreaking reign of God, just as Jesus indicated in 9:1. The coming of the kingdom in this passage may not look like the arrival of the eschaton, as many have supposed from Jesus's prediction in 9:1, but we must conclude that the appearance of Moses and Elijah, accompanied by a transfigured Jesus and the voice and presence of God provide us with a clear example of the "kingdom of God coming with power."

We must allow our understanding of the kingdom in Mark to be formed by the narrative itself rather than by the preconceived ideas that we bring to the text. When we allow our imagination to be guided by Mark's distinctive presentation, his vision of the kingdom of God emerges with greater clarity. As stated above, the kingdom is a complex and layered theme in Mark's Gospel. Jesus, the Messiah and Son of God, has come to earth to inaugurate God's reign. His very presence is a sign that a new era has begun that holds promise for the redemption of humanity. But the manifestations of the kingdom that we witness in Jesus's teaching and ministry activities are just a foretaste of what humanity will experience in the fully consummated reign of God. Jesus offers a preview of the kingdom in both subtle and explicit ways. As we might expect from a powerful God, there are numerous instances in Mark where the inbreaking reign of God emerges with immediacy and power. Having considered these instances, we turn now in chapter 6 to the related motifs of mystery and secrecy that also attend the Gospel's presentation of the reign of God. Once we have completed our consideration of the kingdom in Mark, we will be in a better position to summarize the importance of this theme for Mark's wider theological agenda.

FOR FURTHER READING

A. Greek Grammar and Syntax in Mark

Decker, Rodney J. *Mark 1–8: A Handbook on the Greek Text*. Baylor
    Handbook on the Greek New Testament. Waco, TX: Baylor
    University Press, 2014.

Decker, Rodney J. *Mark 9–16: A Handbook on the Greek Text*. Baylor
    Handbook on the Greek New Testament. Waco, TX: Baylor
    University Press, 2015.

Decker, Rodney J. "Markan Idiolect in the Study of the Greek of
    the New Testament." In *The Language of the New Testament:
    Context, History, and Development*, edited by Stanley E. Porter
    and Andrew W. Pitts, 43–66. ECHC 3. Leiden: Brill, 2013.

Maloney, Elliott C. *Semitic Interference in Marcan Syntax*. SBLDS 51.
    Atlanta: Society of Biblical Literature, 1981.

Vorster, W. S. "Bilingualism and the Greek of the New Testament:
    Semitic Interference in the Gospel of Mark." *Neot* 24.2 (1990):
    215–28.

B. Healings and Exorcisms in Mark

Cotter, Wendy J. *The Christ of the Miracle Stories: Portrait Through
    Encounter*. Grand Rapids: Baker Academic, 2010.

Cotter, Wendy J. *Miracles in Greco-Roman Antiquity: A Sourcebook for
    the Study of New Testament Miracle Stories*. The Context of Early
    Christianity. New York: Routledge, 1999.

Twelftree, Graham H. *In the Name of Jesus: Exorcism Among Early
    Christians*. Grand Rapids: Baker Academic, 2007.

Twelftree, Graham H. *Jesus the Exorcist: A Contribution to the Study
    of the Historical Jesus*. WUNT 2.54. Tübingen: Mohr Siebeck,
    1993.

Twelftree, Graham H. *Jesus the Miracle Worker: A Historical and
    Theological Study*. Downers Grove: InterVarsity Press, 1999.

C. Purity Concerns in Mark's Social and Religious Contexts

Klawans, Jonathan. *Impurity and Sin in Ancient Judaism*. Oxford:
    Oxford University Press, 2000.

Thiessen, Matthew. *Jesus and the Forces of Death: The Gospels' Portrayal of Ritual Impurity Within First-Century Judaism*. Grand Rapids: Baker Academic, 2021.

D. Intercalations in Mark

Downing, F. Gerald. *Doing Things with Words in the First Christian Century*. JSNTSup 200. Sheffield: Sheffield Academic Press, 2000. See chapter 6, "Markan Intercalation in Cultural Context," 118–32.

Edwards, James R. "Markan Sandwiches: The Significance of Interpolations in Markan Narratives." *NovT* 31.1 (1989): 193–216.

Hatton, Stephen B. "Comic Ambiguity in the Markan Healing Intercalation (Mark 5:21–43)." *Neot* 49.1 (2015): 91–123.

Proctor, Mark A. "'It Was Not the Season for Figs': Aesthetic Absurdity in Mark's Intercalations." *Bib* 98.4 (2017): 558–81.

Shepherd, Tom. *Markan Sandwich Stories: Narration, Definition, and Function*. Andrews University Seminary Doctoral Dissertation Series 18. Berrien Springs, MI: Andrews University Press, 1993.

Shepherd, Tom. "The Narrative Function of Markan Intercalation." *NTS* 41.4 (1995): 522–40.

Van Oyen, Geert. "Intercalation and Irony in the Gospel of Mark." In *The Four Gospels 1992: Festschrift Frans Neirynck*, edited by F. van Segbroeck, 2.949–74. 3 vols. BETL 100. Leuven: Peeters, 1992.

CHAPTER 6

The Kingdom of God in Mark (Part 2)

Secrecy and the Mysteries of God's Reign

In the previous chapter, we examined Mark's emphasis on the arrival of God's kingdom with immediacy and power. In this chapter, we turn to the proverbial "other side of the coin" to examine how Mark's presentation of the kingdom of God is also cloaked in secrecy, shrouded in mystery, and arrives in the most unexpected ways. In most of the passages considered in the previous chapter, the phrase "kingdom of God" is absent. It is therefore up to the reader to discern the nuances of the wider narrative rhetoric related to Mark's presentation of the inbreaking reign of God. However, if we can learn a great deal about Mark's understanding of the kingdom from those passages in which the phrase "kingdom of God" is absent, it seems prudent—and potentially equally instructive—to examine those texts where Jesus makes specific reference to the kingdom. We begin here with the source of the clearest and most obvious kingdom language in Mark—Jesus's parables.

TO REVEAL AND CONCEAL: MARK'S KINGDOM PARABLES

As noted previously, the phrase "kingdom of God" first appears in Mark 1:14–15, when Jesus begins his public career. Along with casting out unclean spirits, preaching about God's kingdom represents one of the foundational elements of Jesus's public ministry in Mark. The second appearance of kingdom language is in 4:11, just before Jesus offers his explanation of the so-called parable of the sower (4:3–9), and Jesus signals there that his parables are about the mysteries of God's kingdom. Before we consider Jesus's explanation of this parable, several observations are in order. First, to this point in the narrative, Jesus has only spoken in parables in three brief episodes (2:17, 19–22, 25–28), but the narrator has not yet paused to focus attention on their purpose. Thus, the parable of the sower represents the audience's first real exposure to the goal of this type of teaching in the Gospel. Second, this parable also serves as *the paradigmatic example* of how the literary audience should hear, understand, and attempt to interpret Jesus's parables throughout the remainder of the narrative. For broader context, this is one of only two parables in Mark for which an explanation is given, and as the first, it provides some interpretive guidance for the audience.[1]

---

1. The other parable explanation is found in 7:17–23 (NRSVue):

    When he had left the crowd and entered the house, his disciples asked him about the parable. He said to them, "So, are you also without understanding? Do you not see that whatever goes into a person from outside cannot defile, since it enters not the heart but the stomach and goes out into the sewer?" (Thus he declared all foods clean.) And he said, "It is what comes out of a person that defiles. For it is from within, from the human heart, that evil intentions come: sexual immorality, theft, murder, adultery, avarice, wickedness, deceit, debauchery, envy, slander, pride, folly. All these evil things come from within, and they defile a person."

This much seems clear from Jesus's surprise at the inability of the disciples to comprehend what he has said. In response to their ignorance he asks, "Do you not understand *this parable*? Then how will you understand *all the parables*?" (4:13; emphasis added). His explanation proceeds from there.

The parables of Jesus have been an almost constant source of interest for those studying and writing about early Christian gospels, particularly over the last two centuries. One persistent question that has attended scholarly reflection is, "To what extent are the parables allegories?"[2] In the explanation provided by Jesus (4:13–20), we see that some level of allegorizing is necessary to understand the parables. Otherwise, Jesus recounts a rather banal story of a farmer sowing seed widely and indiscriminately. Some of that seed falls on the foot path and is quickly devoured by birds (4:4). Other seed shoots up quickly but lacks the necessary depth of soil to grow organically. When the sun rises, those sprouts are withered (4:5–6). A third soil on which the seed is thrown contains thorns, which grow together with the seed. Those thorns eventually choke out the seed that has been sown (4:7). Finally, the fourth seed falls on good soil and yields a remarkable harvest (4:8). Without the explanation that follows in 4:13–20, this parable appears simply to recount the workaday experience of farmers in Roman Palestine during the first century CE. Those listening to this parable with even

---

2. Allegory is a genre of storytelling in which elements of a story ultimately correspond to some greater reality. Perhaps the most famous and straightforward example of allegory in Christian writing is John Bunyan's book *The Pilgrim's Progress*. A more subtle allegory is C. S. Lewis's *The Lion, the Witch and the Wardrobe*, in which Aslan the Lion represents Jesus, the White Witch represents Satan, and their battle over Narnia represents God's war for the souls of humanity. For a broader discussion on the question of allegory and other important introductory concerns related to interpreting Jesus's parables, see Klyne Snodgrass, *Stories with Intent: A Comprehensive Guide to the Parables of Jesus*, 2nd ed. (Grand Rapids: Eerdmans, 2018), 1–36.

a cursory knowledge of farming would have had an immediate frame of reference for understanding what Jesus has
just described, but in a first-century Palestinian context, the
story itself is not terribly interesting or novel. Thus, to make
sense of the parable, the narrative audience must rely on the
interpretation Jesus provides—an explanation not everyone
is privileged to receive.

Jesus explains that the different soils represent people in
their various responses to God's word. The first soil represents
an individual who receives the word and has it immediately
stolen away. The birds that devour the soil along the footpath
correspond to Satan, who quickly steals the word that was
sown in them (4:15). Just as the second, rocky soil lacks depth,
so does the person who joyfully receives God's word but then
falls away on account of trouble or persecution (4:16–17). The
third seed sown among thorns corresponds to those people
who receive the word but eventually succumb to wealth and
the cares of life. Just as the weeds choke out any growth from
the soil, the trappings of this life stifle any growth from such
an individual (4:18–19). Finally, and perhaps most predictably, the fruitful soil with its various harvests of thirty, sixty,
and one hundredfold, represents those who hear the word,
persist in it, and grow bountifully.

Note that, along with the literary audience, *only those
within the narrative who are considered insiders* are privy to the
explanation of this parable. In fact, in 4:11–12, Jesus explicitly indicates to his disciples and the others gathered around
him that he intends to speak the mysteries of God's kingdom
openly to them while actively seeking to conceal the message
from those on the outside:

> And he said to them, "To you [plural] has been given the
> secret of the kingdom of God, *but for those outside everything*

comes in parables, in order that 'they may indeed look but
not perceive, and may indeed hear but not understand; so
that they may not turn again and be forgiven.'" (4:11–12
NRSVue; emphasis added)[3]

Here we have another narrative moment of critical importance, and it will inform not only our understanding of
Jesus's parables but also Mark's presentation of the kingdom
throughout the rest of the text. Read plainly, Jesus appears
to be saying that he speaks in mysterious parables with the
goal of *concealing the truths of God's kingdom from the masses.*
Only those on the "inside" are privileged to hear Jesus speak
openly about these mysteries. Just in case we are tempted
to regard this as the only parable explanation to which the
disciples have access, Mark clarifies in 4:33–34: "With many
such parables he spoke the word to [the crowds], as they were
able to hear it; he did not speak to them except in parables,
but he explained everything in private to his disciples" (emphasis
added).

What are we to make of this? Mark's Jesus intends to
reveal the truths of the kingdom to his disciples and conceal them from the crowds? If Jesus is both Messiah and
Son of God, should he not, above all, want the masses—the
"outsiders"—to comprehend the mysteries of the kingdom
and turn to God? On initial reading, this does not appear
to be the case, but as indicated in the previous chapter, it is
important for us to allow Mark's presentation, rather than

---

3. Jesus is quoting an abbreviated version of Isa 6:9–10 here: And he said,
"Go and say to this people: 'Keep listening, but do not comprehend; keep looking, but do not understand.' Make the mind of this people dull, and stop their
ears, and shut their eyes, so that they may not look with their eyes, and listen with
their ears, and comprehend with their minds, and turn and be healed." We will
see that Mark's Jesus uses this quotation a bit differently than it originally appears
in Isaiah.

our preconceived ideas, to shape our understanding of the kingdom of God.

Much ink has been spilled over Mark 4:11–12, some of which has attempted to pivot the discussion to later developing theological doctrines such as predestination, election, or the extent of the atonement. However, such explanations do little to clarify how Jesus's words fit within the broader narrative rhetoric of Mark's Gospel. If we read 4:11–12 and then trace the trajectory of those who comprehend the mysteries of the kingdom and those who do not across the entire Gospel, we will find that the opposite of what Jesus announces occurs. Those to whom these truths are revealed—the disciples—descend into seemingly greater levels of incomprehension until, at the very end of the Gospel, they are bereft of both hope and understanding and they all abandon Jesus without being rehabilitated.[4] By contrast, from this point in the narrative, various figures from whom these kingdom truths are concealed unexpectedly understand, respond in faith, and even occasionally surprise Jesus.

It is worth pausing here to explore this contrast in greater detail. The disciples are the ultimate insiders. They are privy to Jesus's miracles, exorcisms, and parables and their explanations. Thus, our expectation is that they should grow progressively in their ability to comprehend truths about the kingdom: Jesus's identity and purpose, the mission before them, and God's way of working in the world. However, that is not what transpires. Throughout the course of the narrative, the disciples consistently miss the point. Consider the following examples:

---

4. The incomprehension of the disciples has long been a topic of discussion among scholars. We will discuss this in greater detail in chapter 7. It is important to point out here that the presentation of the disciples in Mark consists of both positive and negative depictions.

1. *"Who is this man?" (4:35–41):* Just after we are told that Jesus explained everything to his disciples in private (4:33–34), the entire group gets into a boat on the Sea of Galilee, and a huge storm arises (4:35–37). While the disciples are in fear for their lives, Jesus is asleep at the stern (4:38). Once he is awakened, Jesus first rebukes the wind and the sea, commanding them to be still and silent (4:39). He then turns to the astonished disciples and castigates them for their lack of faith (4:40). Their collective response is telling: "And they were filled with great awe and said to one another, 'Who then is this, that even the wind and the sea obey him?'" (4:41). Presumably they already know who Jesus is since they have been following him for some time. Also, why wake him up if they are not anticipating some action on his part? Jesus's question about their lack of faith is our first signal that the Twelve do not fully comprehend Jesus's message, mission, and identity.

2. *"How can we feed these people?" (8:1–10):* In Mark 6:30–44, Jesus feeds a multitude of five thousand men by multiplying five barley loaves and two small fish. In 8:1, we encounter another great crowd—this time four thousand (8:9)—that has been with Jesus for three days with nothing to eat (8:1–2). Jesus expresses concern about sending them away because they may faint from hunger on their way home, especially since some have traveled a very long way (8:3). In 8:4, the disciples respond: "How can one feed these people with bread here in the desert?" This would be a legitimate question if they had not already witnessed Jesus feed an even larger multitude with meager rations just two chapters earlier. Their unqualified question is another signal to

the literary audience that the Twelve are characterized by an inability to understand Jesus.

3. *"We have no bread!"* (8:14–21): Just after the second miraculous provision of food, Jesus and the disciples enter the boat, and the narrator indicates that the disciples neglected to bring any bread with them (8:14)—presumably the bread in question is that which is left over from the previous scene. On the heels of this statement from the narrator, Jesus begins to warn the Twelve about the "yeast of the Pharisees and the yeast of Herod" (8:15). The disciples mistakenly believe that Jesus is speaking about yeast, not metaphorically but literally, because they have failed to bring bread into the boat (8:16). We can get a sense of Jesus's exasperation at their incomprehension in the series of rapid-fire questions with which he confronts them:

- "Why are you talking about having no bread?" (8:17)
- "Do you still not perceive or understand?" (8:17)
- "Are your hearts hardened?" (8:17)
- "Do you have eyes, and fail to see?" (8:18)
- "Do you have ears, and fail to hear?" (8:18)
- "And do you not remember?" (8:18)
- "Do you not yet understand?" (8:21)

These questions betray the disciples' ongoing struggle to comprehend the significance of Jesus's words and actions. As we will see below, the situation only worsens from here.

4. *"Get behind me Satan!"* (8:27–33): In 8:27, at the beginning of the so-called turning point in Mark's Gospel,

Jesus enters a brief conversation with his disciples in which they discuss the various ways that those on the outside have identified him. They respond with a handful of options: John the Baptist, Elijah, one of the prophets (8:28). When Jesus poses that same question to the Twelve, Peter responds with a partially correct answer: "You are the Messiah" (8:29). After ordering them to keep this a secret, Jesus begins to discuss his imminent death at the hands of the religious leaders and his resurrection after three days (8:31); this is the first of three such predictions (cf. also 9:31, 10:32–34). In keeping with our emphasis on the disciples as insiders, Mark includes an important comment in 8:32: "He said all this quite openly." By now, this has become a theme in the Gospel. Jesus speaks openly and plainly to his disciples, and by this point in their experiences with him, the Twelve should be attuned to the nuances of his message about the kingdom and its agenda, and they should respond affirmatively. However, Peter takes Jesus aside and begins to rebuke him (8:32), which prompts Jesus to respond: "Get behind me, Satan! For you are setting your mind not on divine things but on human things" (8:33). This shocking scene occurs just after Peter's "big moment"—his confession that Jesus is the Messiah—something the audience has known since 1:1. Peter is often regarded as the leader and mouthpiece of the Twelve, and as such, he represents their collective understanding. His confession of Jesus as the Messiah should be a moment of triumph, but instead, this scene ends in rebuke. While Peter has correctly identified *that* Jesus is the Messiah, he does not fully appreciate *what* that means or *how* Jesus's messiahship will unfold. Therefore, he rejects Jesus's teaching about his death and resurrection. What it means for Mark's Jesus to be the Messiah, at least in part, is that he must give his life a ransom for many (10:45). His role as Christ and Son of God is intimately connected to his death and resurrection, which is a far cry from the various messianic expectations operative at the time.[5]

5. ***Who will be the greatest in the kingdom? (9:30–37):*** As Jesus and the Twelve are passing through Galilee, Jesus predicts for a second time that he will be handed over and killed (9:31). Once the group reaches Capernaum (9:33), Jesus asks the disciples about the conversation they had on the road. The Twelve are unwilling to reveal to him the substance of their discussion, because they had been debating who among them would be greatest in the fully realized reign of God (9:33–34). Their debate shows a failure to reckon with Jesus's earlier prediction of his imminent death (8:31) as well as the emphasis on service that lies at the heart of his vocation. The disciples have miscalculated as they are focusing too much on the acclaim that has accrued to Jesus—and likely to them as a result—and have lost sight of one of the major emphases of Jesus's ministry. Jesus will make his role as servant even clearer in the coming chapter (cf. 10:32–34; 45). For now, this miscalculation is yet more evidence that the Markan disciples are characterized by a spiritual dullness and inability to comprehend the most important truths connected with Jesus and his public ministry.

---

5. As discussed in chapter 3, we have no evidence from this period of any Jewish messianic expectation that also included the violent death of the Messiah. By contrast, the very concept of Messiah implies victory. The notion of a crucified Messiah was a troublesome paradox for early Christians, especially against the backdrop of the various messianic ideas in the first century CE.

While these are not the only examples of the disciples' failure in the Gospel of Mark, they suffice to demonstrate a consistent pattern: the ultimate insiders, those to whom the mysteries of God's kingdom have been revealed, fail to understand the message and mission of Jesus.[6] By contrast, several individuals in the Gospel come to understand kingdom truths that have been obscured or concealed from them. In these moments, the audience learns something critical about the nature of God's kingdom: it is available to outsiders, to those on the margins, and to those we might least expect to understand and turn to God.

Perhaps the most conspicuous example of this phenomenon is found in one of the passages we considered in the previous chapter: Mark 7:24–30. This text represents a rare example in which both the immediacy and power of God's kingdom and its mysterious emergence are simultaneously on display. Turning to the story once again, we read:

> From there he set out and went away to the region of Tyre. He entered a house and did not want anyone to know he was there. Yet he could not escape notice, but a woman whose little daughter had an unclean spirit immediately heard about him, and she came and bowed down at his feet. Now the woman was a gentile, of Syrophoenician origin. She begged him to cast the demon out of her daughter. He said to her, "Let the children be fed first, for it is not fair to take the children's food and throw it to the dogs." But she answered him, "Sir, even the dogs

---

6. For other examples of the failure and incomprehension of the disciples, see 9:14–29 (they are unable to cast out a demon); 10:35–40 (the sons of Zebedee seek seats of honor in the coming kingdom); 14:10–11, 18–21, 41–46 (Judas betrays Jesus); 14:29–31, 66–72 (Peter denies knowing Jesus three times); and 14:50–52 (the disciples all flee, abandoning Jesus).

under the table eat the children's crumbs." Then he said to her, "For saying that, you may go—the demon has left your daughter." And when she went home, she found the child lying on the bed and the demon gone. (7:24–30 NRSVue)

It is important to note that the conversation between Jesus and the Syrophoenician woman consists of a plea on her part followed by a rather insulting parable on the part of Jesus. The woman responds by entering the world of that parable with an uncompromising resolve that effectively reiterates her initial request. The woman's brave recalcitrance appears to spring Jesus from the world of the parable back into the real world, at which point he grants her request. What is it about this interaction that represents the emergence of the kingdom in a mysterious or counterintuitive way?

The woman that we meet in this text stands in contrast to the disciples in nearly every important respect. She is a woman. The Twelve are all men. She is a gentile. The Twelve are all Jews. She is unnamed. Each of the Twelve has been introduced to the audience by name (cf. 3:13–19). She has not been privy to the formal explanation of any of Jesus's parables, while the Twelve have had everything explained directly to them. From all outward signs, there is nothing about this woman that would signal her ability to (1) comprehend the parable Jesus utters, (2) respond in a meaningful way, or (3) receive the thing for which she has petitioned Jesus. But she defies most, if not all, of our expectations.

Earlier in the narrative, Jesus provides a parable that might give us some insight into figures like the Syrophoenician woman:

With what can we compare the kingdom of God, or what parable will we use for it? It is like a mustard seed, which, when sown upon the ground, is the smallest of all the seeds on earth; yet when it is sown it grows up and becomes the greatest of all shrubs, and puts forth large branches, so that the birds of the air can make nests in its shade. (4:30–32)

According to Jesus, the kingdom is like a tiny, unimpressive mustard seed. Outside the world of ancient horticulture, few who observe the seemingly insignificant seed could predict that it would eventually grow into something so enormous with such a distinct purpose. Those who are tempted to judge the quality of that seed or its ability to become something great have underestimated its potential. In other words, God's kingdom is not constrained by outward appearances of size, strength, value, or significance. In the same way, readers might be tempted to judge this anonymous, gentile woman as unimpressive or insignificant, but her ability to comprehend Jesus's parable, respond in faith, and receive the thing she has requested shows that God's reign emerges in unexpected and counterintuitive ways. Thus, God's kingdom is not just for those on the inside, but also, and perhaps most importantly, for *those on the outside and those on the margins.*

FIGURE 6.1

Does Jesus Insult the Syrophoenician Woman?

Given that Jesus stands at the center of a faith tradition for many people, some are understandably troubled by the suggestion that he would intentionally insult someone. In this passage, however, the Markan Jesus uses an insulting term (7:28, "little dogs"; Greek *kynaria*) that we know Jews reserved as a slur toward non-Jews. We must read this text in its wider context, which deals with (1) the feeding of "Israel" (6:31–44), (2) their rejection of Jesus's new way, and (3) early Jewish-Christian anxiety about the role of gentiles in the nascent Christian church.

About this text, Moloney writes:

We must appreciate the subtlety and strength of the Markan rhetoric in this encounter. Having walked away from an arrogant Israel (v. 24; see vv. 1–23), Jesus initially perseveres with the theme of 6:31–44: he gives bread to Israel. He insists that "the children," Israel, be fed first, claiming that it is improper to take that bread and cast it to the Gentiles ("the dogs"). But the reader is aware that Israel has been fed "first.". . . But the response of "the children" has been an arrogant rejection of Jesus' new law of freedom (vv. 1–23). . . . Coming hard upon the heels of Israel's rejection of Jesus' offer of bread, the woman accepts that she is a "dog," and that she must place herself second. . . . In her nothingness, she comes with a complete openness to Jesus. . . . The contrast between Israel's response to Jesus (7:1–23) and the response of the Gentile Syrophoenician woman (7:24–30) could not be more stark. (Francis J. Moloney, *The Gospel of Mark: A Commentary* [Peabody, MA: Hendrickson, 2002], 147.)

A second example appears in Mark 12. That chapter consists of a series of disputes between Jesus and different groups of Jewish authorities. After he utters the so-called parable of the wicked tenants (12:1–12)—a parable aimed at criticizing Jewish leaders—Jesus is then challenged by the Pharisees and Herodians (12:13–17), then by the Sadducees (12:18–27), before entering a conversation with one of the scribes:

> One of the scribes came near and heard them disputing with one another, and seeing that he answered them well, he asked him, "Which commandment is the first of all?" Jesus answered, "The first is, 'Hear, O Israel: the Lord our God, the Lord is one; you shall love the Lord your God with all your heart and with all your soul and with all your mind and with all your strength.' The second is this, 'You shall love your neighbor as yourself.' There is no other commandment greater than these." Then the scribe said to him, "You are right, Teacher; you have truly said that 'he is one, and besides him there is no other'; and 'to love him with all the heart, and with all the understanding, and with all the strength,' and 'to love one's neighbor as oneself'—this is much more important than all whole burnt offerings and sacrifices." When Jesus saw that he answered wisely, he said to him, "You are not far from the kingdom of God." After that no one dared to ask him any question. (12:28–34)

As mentioned above, this conversation between Jesus and the scribe results directly from the dispute occasioned by the parable of the wicked tenants (12:28). In the heated context of these disputes between Jesus and the religious authorities, we unexpectedly encounter a scribe who, after initially challenging Jesus, approvingly reiterates Jesus's answer to his question (12:32–33a) and then expands on the answer with his own interpretive comment: "this is much more important than all whole burnt offerings and sacrifices" (12:33b). The narrator identifies this comment as "wise," after which Jesus responds, "You are not far from the kingdom of God." This is an unexpected response since (1) the interactions between Jesus and these various Jewish groups have taken on an increasingly adversarial tone, and (2) the previous two conversations, first with the Pharisees and Herodians (12:13–17) and then with the Sadducees (12:18–27), both ended on a dismissive note. Those conversations centered on the interpretation of the Hebrew Scriptures and in both, Jesus arrives at a different conclusion from his interlocuters. In this third scene, however, the scribe is able to see beyond any potential parochial interpretive issues that might separate him and Jesus, and he embraces not only the direct teaching of the Torah but some of its major social and religious implications. Once again, an outsider, from whom kingdom truths have been concealed, responds to Jesus in a way that upends Jesus's words in 4:11–12.[7]

The point of this focused consideration of kingdom mysteries, especially for insiders and outsiders, is that when truths are discovered by those from whom Jesus seeks to conceal them, the kingdom of God is present. Or, to say it differently, those who manifest faith despite having the message concealed from them are, in the words of Jesus, "not far from the kingdom." In Mark's Gospel, being an insider or outsider is not a function of physical proximity to Jesus, nor is it directly related one's gender, nationality, or present

---

7. In what is perhaps the most striking example of an outsider's recognition of Jesus, the centurion—a Roman solider participating in the crucifixion—announces that he is the "Son of God" (15:39). As noted in chapter 4, this epiphany is significant for a number of reasons.

religious commitments. Rather, being (or perhaps, *becoming*) an insider is all about comprehending the essence of Jesus's mission and displaying a willingness to follow. The Markan Jesus thus demolishes the outward standards by which "insiders" and "outsiders" would have been identified and creates a new set of standards defined by the ability to discern truth and follow God.

SECRECY AND THE KINGDOM OF GOD

One of the distinctive literary and theological features of the Second Gospel is Mark's "secrecy motif." Intimately connected to the discussion of the mysteries of the kingdom is the consistent and variegated presence of secrecy throughout Jesus's ministry. It is also one of the most potentially confusing motifs in the Gospel. Mark provides us with an ironic portrait of a professed messiah figure who goes out of his way to keep his identity from being revealed. This motif manifests itself in a number of ways throughout the public ministry of Jesus, including (1) his not allowing demons to speak (e.g., 1:25, 34; 3:12), (2) his commands to silence both during and after his deeds of power (e.g., 1:44–45; 5:43; 7:35–36), and (3) his various attempts at maintaining anonymity (e.g., 8:30; 9:9).

The first to identify this motif was the German scholar William Wrede in his important book *The Messianic Secret*.[8] Wrede, along with other representatives of the History of Religions school, approached the Gospel as if it provided a historical "window" through which we might gain authentic

---

8. The book first appeared in 1901 under the German title *Das Messiasgeheimnis in den Evangelien: Zugleich ein Beitrag zum Verständnis des Markusevangeliums*, which translates to *The Messiah-Secret in the Gospels: At the Same Time a Contribution to the Study of the Gospel of Mark*. The first English edition appeared seventy years later under the title *The Messianic Secret*, trans. J. C. G. Greig (Cambridge: James Clarke & Co., 1971).

access to the life of Jesus and his disciples. He saw the smaller components that made up the larger secrecy motif as part of a unified theme across the narrative. As far as Wrede was concerned, Jesus never claimed to be Messiah during his lifetime, even though the Gospel of Mark is concerned to show its audience otherwise. Therefore, the misunderstandings of the disciples and Jesus's commands to secrecy are both later literary creations meant to explain why the disciples never recognized Jesus as the Messiah during his lifetime. While we have Wrede to thank for shining a light on this Markan motif, it is important to note that nearly all contemporary scholars reject his conclusions and have offered different explanations for why the motif exists and how it functions within the Gospel.

To appreciate the various contours of this motif, we need to examine some of the critical passages in which secrecy is a prominent feature. These texts fall into the categories of (1) exorcisms, (2) healings, and (3) Jesus's attempts at safeguarding anonymity. In all three scenarios, secrecy is essential to the developing narrative rhetoric, especially in two areas—Jesus's messianic status and the Gospel's treatment of the kingdom. We turn now to a consideration of important examples of this motif.

Exorcism and Silence

At the outset of Jesus's public ministry, we witness a series of rapidly unfolding scenes depicting his programmatic activity: preaching and teaching (1:14–15, 38–39a), exorcisms (1:21–28; 34b, 39b), and healings (1:29–34a, 40–45). These scenes are paradigmatic for the audience. They introduce us to the routine ministry activities of Jesus while also including his regular practice of commanding silence during displays of power and moments of epiphany. These scenes set the stage for what will continue to occur at various turns throughout the rest of the Gospel. Since we have already discussed Jesus's regular practice of exorcism in the previous chapter, we do not need to cover that ground here. What we left unaddressed in our prior discussion of exorcisms in Mark, however, is the role secrecy and the silencing of the demonic play in those power encounters. Before we analyze this motif, let us first consider three textual examples.

1. *Mark 1:21–28:* "They went to Capernaum; and when the sabbath came, he entered the synagogue and taught. They were astounded at his teaching, for he taught them as one having authority, and not as the scribes. Just then there was in their synagogue a man with an unclean spirit, and he cried out, 'What have you to do with us, Jesus of Nazareth? Have you come to destroy us? I know who you are, the Holy One of God.' But Jesus rebuked him, saying, *'Be silent, and come out of him!'* And the unclean spirit, convulsing him and crying with a loud voice, came out of him. They were all amazed, and they kept on asking one another, 'What is this? A new teaching—with authority! He commands even the unclean spirits, and they obey him.' At once his fame began to spread throughout the surrounding region of Galilee" (emphasis added).

2. *Mark 1:32–34:* "That evening, at sundown, they brought to him all who were sick or possessed with demons. And the whole city was gathered around the door. And he cured many who were sick with various diseases, and cast out many demons; *and he would not permit the demons to speak, because they knew him*" (emphasis added).

3. *Mark 3:9–12:* "He told his disciples to have a boat ready for him because of the crowd, so that they would not crush him; for he had cured many, so that all who had diseases pressed upon him to touch him. Whenever the unclean spirits saw him, they fell down before him and shouted, 'You are the Son of God!' *But he sternly ordered them not to make him known*" (emphasis added).

In each of the above texts, Jesus encounters demons/unclean spirits who are capable of recognizing him and proclaiming his unique status as God's Son. As a result, Jesus commands them to silence. Within the world of the text, this observation is important for several reasons. First, there is an ironic dimension to this phenomenon. Demonic forces are representatives of Satan, Jesus's chief opponent in the Gospel, yet they are among the figures who most commonly identify Jesus correctly. We cannot even say this about the human figures in the Gospel, including his disciples!

Second, the scenario in which unclean spirits have the potential to speak Jesus's name and ascribe to him some sort of honorific reflects a belief that existed within the ancient contexts in which Mark emerged; this belief is directly related to the ascription of one's name. George Ramsey has noted that it is commonly observed in studies of the Hebrew Bible "that the act of bestowing a name on a person or a place is a demonstration of authority over that person or place."[9] In

---

9. George Ramsey, "Is Name-Giving an Act of Domination in Genesis 2:23 and Elsewhere?," *CBQ* 50.1 (1988): 24–35 (here 25). Another interesting example of this phenomenon occurs in the narrative of Marduk's birth in the *Enuma Elish*, where Ea gives him his name as well as the introduction to the list of names. By being given the names of other gods, the text is suggesting that Marduk is taking on their very identity. On this, see Andrea Seri, "The Fifty Names of Marduk in *Enūma eliš*," *JAOS* 126.4 (2006): 507–19. The idea also appears with the god Ninurta in the *Epic of Anzû*. I am grateful to Dr. Raleigh Heth for these insights and for his pointing me to other textual examples of this phenomenon.

other words, name-giving in ancient Near Eastern literature was often an exercise in power, domination, or control. We see this, for instance, in stories where humans encounter members of the angelic realm and the giving of one's name is understood as a transfer of power (e.g., Gen 32:27–29; cf. Mark 5:9). In these power encounters with Jesus, the unclean spirits correctly recognize him and are ready to proclaim his identity openly. In fact, in Mark 1:24, the demoniac professes that he is "Jesus of Nazareth . . . the Holy One of God" before being silenced. In subsequent interactions the unclean spirits are not even allowed to speak, except for when Jesus is directly addressing them (cf. 5:8–12). The inability of the demoniacs to call Jesus by name or even speak not only is a reflection of Jesus's supreme power over that realm but is further indication that his defeat of Satan was proleptically secured during his time in the wilderness (cf. 1:12–13). In these instances, the silencing of demoniacs is (1) a demonstration of Jesus's power, (2) further confirmation for the audience that what the narrator affirmed about Jesus in 1:1–15 is true, and (3) a signal of the inbreaking reign of God in the here and now. For our purposes in this chapter, the third consideration is most pertinent.

In these encounters, we witness the power of God on display through Jesus, and this power is but a small part of the larger reality that is God's reign on earth. The secrecy motif is principally about Christology, but we cannot doubt that it is also connected to the broader theme of the emergence of God's kingdom on earth. In the exorcism stories, secrecy, Christology, and the mysteries of God's reign are intimately intertwined. God's reign in Mark is characterized by power over Satan and his demonic emissaries. Jesus, the Messiah and Son of God, was able to secure an initial victory in the wilderness (cf. 1:12–13) and the ripple effects of this victory are continually displayed throughout the remainder of the narrative. Thus, it should not surprise us that these demonic forces are capable of immediately recognizing Jesus for who he is. Nor should it surprise us that he is able to silence them so easily. The reason for this silencing, however, may be surprising for some readers. For Mark, Jesus has come, not to be proclaimed as king, but to suffer on the cross and be raised by God's power. Thus, it is necessary to silence those who would make him known, at least for the time being. We will see this emphasis even more prominently in our next section.

Healing and Secrecy

Other important instances of secrecy in the Gospel appear in Jesus's practice of ordering individuals and crowds to be silent about the miraculous events they have witnessed. From a literary perspective, this is potentially more confusing than Jesus commanding the unclean spirits to silence. We see this phenomenon in the following examples.

1. *Mark 1:40–45:* "A leper came to him begging him, and kneeling he said to him, 'If you choose, you can make me clean.' Moved with pity, Jesus stretched out his hand and touched him, and said to him, 'I do choose. Be made clean!' Immediately the leprosy left him, and he was made clean. *After sternly warning him he sent him away at once, saying to him, 'See that you say nothing to anyone; but go, show yourself to the priest, and offer for your cleansing what Moses commanded, as a testimony to them.'* But he went out and began to proclaim it freely, and to spread the word, so that Jesus could no longer go into a town openly, but stayed out in the country; and people came to him from every quarter" (emphasis added).

2. *Mark 5:39–43:* "When he had entered, he said to them, 'Why do you make a commotion and weep? The child is not dead but sleeping.' And they laughed at him. Then he put them all outside, and took the child's father and mother and those who were with him, and went in where the child was. He took her by the hand and said to her, 'Talitha cum,' which means, 'Little girl, get up!' And immediately the girl got up and began to walk about (she was twelve years of age). At this they were overcome with amazement. *He strictly ordered them that no one should know this, and told them to give her something to eat*" (emphasis added).

3. *Mark 7:31–37:* "Then he returned from the region of Tyre, and went by way of Sidon towards the Sea of Galilee, in the region of the Decapolis. They brought to him a deaf man who had an impediment in his speech; and they begged him to lay his hand on him. He took him aside in private, away from the crowd, and put his fingers into his ears, and he spat and touched his tongue. Then looking up to heaven, he sighed and said to him, 'Ephphatha,' that is, 'Be opened.' And immediately his ears were opened, his tongue was released, and he spoke plainly. *Then Jesus ordered them to tell no one; but the more he ordered them, the more zealously they proclaimed it.* They were astounded beyond measure, saying, 'He has done everything well; he even makes the deaf to hear and the mute to speak'" (emphasis added).

These encounters raise a number of questions: (1) Why does Jesus want the crowds to remain silent about his deeds? (2) How realistic is such an expectation? and (3) What do these instances contribute to our understanding of the broader secrecy motif and its connection to the mysterious reign of God?

First, without an appreciation of Mark's Christology, our initial question would be difficult to answer. However, in chapters 2 and 3, I have provided a detailed consideration of Mark's christological presentation. For Mark, Jesus is the Messiah and Son of God, but he fulfills both of these roles in a way that upends some the dominant religious and civic expectations of the time. Mark's Jesus has come, "not to be served but to serve, and to give his life a ransom for many" (10:45). These commands to silence are intended to keep Jesus's messianic fame from spreading, but we see that this fails miserably. In fact, the more Jesus commands the crowds to silence, the more they proclaim what they have seen.[10] Mark notes that Jesus's renown spreads so widely that he can no longer enter public spaces without being noticed (1:45).

Second, given the details of the text and our own understanding of human nature, we must admit that Jesus's commands to secrecy appear to be somewhat unrealistic. How likely is it that an individual or group could witness something like the miracles described in the Gospel and then remain silent about it? How could any of us be silent about witnessing something so spectacular? This is confirmed by the fact that virtually no one obeys Jesus when he sternly commands them to silence.

Third, I have already made the case that we cannot understand the kingdom of God in Mark without an appreciation for Jesus's mission and identity. In turn, one cannot understand Jesus's mission and identity apart from his death and resurrection. These themes are interconnected in the

---

10. There is an interesting reversal of this pattern in 16:1–8, where the women are finally told to proclaim the message openly and they say nothing to anyone out of fear (16:8).

healing narratives and further reinforce Mark's presentation of the mysteriousness of God's reign.

Anonymity and Concealment

In one final set of texts, we need to examine instances in the Gospel in which Jesus tries to maintain his anonymity.

1. *Mark 8:27–30:* "Jesus went on with his disciples to the villages of Caesarea Philippi; and on the way he asked his disciples, 'Who do people say that I am?' And they answered him, 'John the Baptist; and others, Elijah; and still others, one of the prophets.' He asked them, 'But who do you say that I am?' Peter answered him, 'You are the Messiah.' *And he sternly ordered them not to tell anyone about him*" (emphasis added).

2. *Mark 9:9–10:* "As they were coming down the mountain, *he ordered them to tell no one about what they had seen*, until after the Son of Man had risen from the dead. So they kept the matter to themselves, questioning what this rising from the dead could mean" (emphasis added).

Again we ask, why is Jesus so concerned to keep his identity a secret? As with the previous two sets of texts, we continue to affirm the connection between Jesus's identity and mission and its connection to the inbreaking reign of God. These two elements go hand in hand in Mark's Gospel and cannot be separated.

Jesus, the Messiah and Son of God has come to serve, to give his life as a ransom for many. During his earthly ministry, he is a conduit for the inbreaking of God's reign on the earth, but only in an embryonic way. What we experience in these stories is a foretaste of the fully realized reign of

God in the eschaton. Thus, while we await the kingdom in its fullness, we are treated to moments of incredible power shrouded in mystery. We witness displays of authority through the messianic kingdom-bringer, whose identity must remain secret so as not to confuse his mission or mistake the end goal of his ministry.

It is important to ponder the question once again, "Why is secrecy critical to Mark's theme of the inbreaking reign of God?" The Markan Jesus has come to inaugurate the kingdom on earth, and we see elements of this inbreaking throughout the Gospel—especially in his numerous encounters with unclean spirits who want to speak his name. But the reality and realm of God's kingdom can only be *fully consummated* by means of Jesus's death and resurrection and his ultimate return. It would be useless, therefore, for some to seize him during his time on earth and attempt to make him king. Thus, secrecy is a necessity for his mission and is therefore a crucial part of Mark's vision of the kingdom of God in the ministry of Jesus.

THE MULTIFACETED, UNPREDICTABLE KINGDOM IN MARK

These past two chapters on the kingdom have sought to emphasize the unpredictable nature of God's inbreaking reign throughout the Gospel of Mark. In some instances, we witness the immediacy and power of God's reign in the manifestations of healing and life that attend miracles, exorcisms, and other deeds of power performed by Jesus. In other instances, we are surprised by events that contradict the way we think things "ought to be." For Mark, God is multifaceted—both powerful and mysterious—and the inbreaking of the kingdom on earth in its various manifestations is a reflection

of that God. This examination shows us that the ways of
God, as least as envisioned by Mark, are inscrutable and
awe-inspiring. Though later Gospel writers will ultimately
incorporate this emphasis, we should regard the reign of God
that is *explicitly available to outsiders* as a distinctively Markan
theme, and one that significantly shapes his presentation of
the Gospel—the *euangelion* of God's emerging kingdom (cf.
1:14–15).

Those who would endeavor to understand, let alone teach
or preach from this enigmatic Gospel must reckon with the
various contours of this theme as it unfolds in Mark. For
Mark, the kingdom is not a paradisaical place in the hereafter reserved for those who have identified with Jesus or
the Christian tradition in some form. Despite contemporary
understandings of the kingdom of God as a future, otherworldly place reserved for God and his righteous saints, we
must recognize that as a much later and less nuanced version
of the kingdom of God. Nor is the kingdom simply the literal
reign of God on earth, though that remains a piece of Mark's
understanding of God's fully consummated reign in the
eschaton. Rather, as Mark envisions it, the specific forms in
which the kingdom of God emerges in the world are unfore-
seeable and manifest themselves in ways that leave us in awe.

Mark's kingdom is a present reality that meets the needs
of the sick, hungry, diseased, and downtrodden in the here
and now, while defying the expectations of those who deem
themselves "worthy." It is also a proleptic projection of how
the world will one day look. In some instances, God's reign
bursts forth into the world with the expected power of an
omnipotent being. In others, it sleeps, then creeps, then
ultimately leaps like the growth of a long-forgotten seed
buried in the ground. In short, the reign of God is reflective
of a mysterious yet loving and caring God, who is chiefly

committed to being a servant of humanity (cf. 10:45). Let these two chapters be an invitation to reflect deeply on the way Mark presents God, Jesus, and the ways in which God's reign is exhibited in the world and in the lives of those with whom Jesus comes into contact.

FOR FURTHER READING

A. Parables of the Markan Jesus

Hultgren, Arland. *The Parables of Jesus: A Commentary.* The Bible in Its World. Grand Rapids: Eerdmans, 2000.

Meier, John P. *A Marginal Jew: Rethinking the Historical Jesus,* vol. 5: *Probing the Authenticity of the Parables.* AYBRL. New Haven, CT: Yale University Press, 2016.

Snodgrass, Klyne. *Stories with Intent: A Comprehensive Guide to the Parables of Jesus.* 2nd ed. Grand Rapids: Eerdmans, 2018.

B. Disciples in Mark

Black, C. Clifton. *The Disciples According to Mark: Markan Redaction in Current Debate.* 2nd ed. Grand Rapids: Eerdmans, 2012.

Carey, Holly J. *Women Who Do: Female Disciples in the Gospels.* Grand Rapids: Eerdmans, 2023. See especially chapter 2, "Female Discipleship in the Gospel of Mark," 48–72.

Danove, Paul L. *The Rhetoric of Characterization of God, Jesus, and Jesus' Disciples in the Gospel of Mark.* JSNTSup 290. London: T&T Clark, 2005. See especially chapter 4, "The Rhetoric of the Characterization of Jesus' Disciples," 90–126.

Malbon, Elizabeth Struthers. *In the Company of Jesus: Characters in Mark's Gospel.* Louisville: Westminster John Knox, 2000. See especially chapter 3, "Disciples/Crowds/Whoever: Markan Characters and Readers," 70–99, and chapter 4, "Text and Contexts: Interpreting the Disciples in Mark," 100–130.

C. Messianic Expectations Within Judaism

Charlesworth, James H., ed. *The Messiah: Developments in Earliest Judaism and Christianity.* Minneapolis: Augsburg Fortress, 1992.

Novenson, Matthew V. *The Grammar of Messianism: An Ancient Jewish Political Idiom and Its Users.* Oxford: Oxford University Press, 2017.

Scholem, Gershom. *The Messianic Idea in Judaism and Other Essays.* New York: Schocken Books, 1995.

D. Mystery in Mark

Dwyer, Timothy. *The Motif of Wonder in the Gospel of Mark.* JSNTSup 128. Sheffield: Sheffield Academic Press, 1996.

Marcus, Joel. *The Mystery of the Kingdom of God.* SBLDS 90. Atlanta: Scholars Press, 1985.

E. Secrecy in Mark

Räisänen, Heikki. *The Messianic Secret in Mark's Gospel.* Studies of the New Testament and Its World. London: T&T Clark, 1990.

Tuckett, Christopher M., ed. *The Messianic Secret.* Issues in Religion and Theology. Minneapolis: Fortress, 1983.

Watson, David F. *Honor Among Christians: The Cultural Key to the Messianic Secret.* Minneapolis: Fortress, 2010.

Wrede, William. *The Messianic Secret.* Translated by J. C. G. Greig. Cambridge: James Clarke & Co., 1971.

CHAPTER 7

Following Jesus on the Way

Discipleship in Mark

Scholars have long noted the prominence of discipleship as a theme in the Second Gospel. Every major section of the narrative begins with a story oriented around the Twelve or the theme of discipleship.

1. After the summary statement in 1:14–15, the section comprising 1:16–3:6 begins with the call of the first disciples (1:16–20).
2. After the summary statement in 3:7–12, the section comprising 3:13–6:6a begins with the choosing by name and commissioning of the Twelve (3:13–19).
3. After the summary statement in 6:6b, the section comprising 6:7–8:30 begins with the sending of the Twelve into their respective ministry activities (6:7–13).
4. The section comprising 8:31–10:52 begins with Jesus predicting his death and Peter rebuking him for this prediction (8:31–33). Additionally, this section is almost solely made up of dialogue between Jesus and the Twelve or other teaching on discipleship.
5. The section comprising 11:1–13:37 begins with Jesus

instructing two of his disciples to find a colt no one
has ever ridden in preparation for his triumphal
entry (11:1–7).
6. The section comprising 14:1–15:47 begins with
Judas's betrayal and is punctuated by Peter's denial
(cf. 14:10, 66–72).

We should also include the last chapter of the Gospel (16:1–8),
which pictures three of Jesus's female followers at the empty
tomb. Their ultimate descent into fear—the note on which
the Gospel ostensibly ends (16:8)—and their emergence out
of fear and into proclamation (which is implied by the very
presence of the story itself) ends the narrative on a note of
discipleship.[1]

We see, then, that stories about the individuals who follow
Jesus during his ministry constitute a prominent narrative
emphasis in Mark, but they represent only one part of a much
wider theme in the Gospel. For our purposes here, Mark's
presentation of discipleship can be broken down into at least
three categories. First, there is formal discipleship language,
including explicit instructions to follow Jesus and to deny
oneself. We also see the metaphorical language of "carrying
one's cross" and pursuing Jesus "on the way." Second, there
is the variegated presentation of the Markan disciples, who

---

1. I recognize that some would dispute my reading of Mark's ending.
However, if we are correct that the Gospel originally ended at 16:8, we must
reckon with the anticlimactic phrase, "They said nothing to anyone, for they were
afraid." This seemingly incomplete ending necessitates that we look beyond the
ending itself. We are led to ask, "If the women remained silent out of fear, how do
we even know the story of their terror and silence?" This, I suggest, is supposed
to be an implicit indication that the women overcame their fear, proclaimed
the resurrection, and followed Jesus. The very fact of their proclamation makes
the Gospel narrative possible. Thus, the enigmatic ending is an implicit call to
discipleship. Readers are to overcome their fear and follow Jesus in the same way
the frightened women chose to face their fear and follow him.

sometimes succeed but more often fail. A great deal has been written on this element of the Gospel. Understanding the role of the Twelve in the Gospel is key to appreciating Mark's overall theology of discipleship. And, third, there is an implicit call to imitate Jesus, a standard feature or expectation of Greco-Roman *bioi*, the genre to which Mark conforms in many ways (as discussed previously); this is overlooked in treatments of discipleship in Mark. Thus, Mark's theology of discipleship is interwoven into the major aspects of the story, including its vocabulary, narrative rhetoric, and choice of genre. Each of these features is examined below.

MARK'S DISCIPLESHIP LANGUAGE

The NT epistolary literature often portrays discipleship as some combination of (a) self-understanding as a follower of Jesus (e.g., 2 Cor 13:5), (b) adherence to certain prescribed behaviors (e.g., Rom 12:1–2; 2 Tim 2:2), and (c) a call to some sort of imitation (e.g. Eph 5:1–2; 1 Cor 11:1). I would argue that these three elements are also present in Mark, but since the Gospel is a narrative rather than a theological treatise, it takes a little more effort to arrive at its understanding of discipleship. Further, Mark's theology oriented around following Jesus is more subtle than those models set forth in the NT epistles, though we do find the occasional use of explicit language related to discipleship. Our examination of Mark's theology of discipleship begins with this unambiguous material and works outward to the more subtle elements of his presentation.

1. *"Come Follow Me"*

The earliest explicit language of discipleship in the Gospel appears in the very first chapter. When Jesus calls his first disciples, the fishermen Peter and Andrew (1:16–18), he commands, "Follow me and I will make you fish for people." At this, they immediately leave their nets and begin to follow him. This action is repeated in 1:19–20, when Jesus calls the sons of Zebedee and they immediately depart from their father's fishing business and follow him. We are not far enough into the narrative to know what all of this means for the full picture of Markan discipleship, but initial indications are that following Jesus entails both a pursuit of others for the sake of the Gospel and a renunciation of one's current life.[2]

2. Doing the Will of God[3]

Another way that Jesus calls those around him to follow is by doing the will of God. This instruction initially appears in the intercalated passage, 3:20–35, where Jesus establishes a new metaphorical "family":

> And the crowd came together again, so that they could not even eat. When his family heard it, they went out to restrain him, for people were saying, "He has gone out of his mind." And the scribes who came down from Jerusalem said, "He has Beelzebul, and by the ruler of the demons he casts out demons." And he called them to him, and spoke

---

2. This pattern continues with Jesus's call of Levi and his immediate departure to follow him in 2:13–14. In 10:28, Peter seems to be aware of the implications of abandoning his life to follow Jesus when he proclaims, "Look, we have left everything and followed you." In response, Jesus says, "Truly I tell you, there is no one who has left house or brothers or sisters or mother or father or children or fields for my sake and for the sake of the good news who will not receive a hundredfold now in this age—houses, brothers and sisters, mothers and children, and fields, with persecutions—and in the age to come eternal life. But many who are first will be last, and the last will be first" (10:29–31 NRSVue).

3. The question of what it means to do the will of God is never directly answered in Mark's Gospel. Instead, we must arrive at our understanding by listening to the commands of Jesus, paying attention to the ways he follows the Father, and trying to emulate those.

to them in parables, "How can Satan cast out Satan? If a kingdom is divided against itself, that kingdom cannot stand. And if a house is divided against itself, that house will not be able to stand. And if Satan has risen up against himself and is divided, he cannot stand, but his end has come. But no one can enter a strong man's house and plunder his property without first tying up the strong man; then indeed the house can be plundered.

"Truly I tell you, people will be forgiven for their sins and whatever blasphemies they utter; but whoever blasphemes against the Holy Spirit can never have forgiveness, but is guilty of an eternal sin"—for they had said, "He has an unclean spirit."

Then his mother and his brothers came; and standing outside, they sent to him and called him. A crowd was sitting around him; and they said to him, "Your mother and your brothers and sisters are outside, asking for you." And he replied, "Who are my mother and my brothers?" *And looking at those who sat around him, he said, "Here are my mother and my brothers! Whoever does the will of God is my brother and sister and mother."* (3:20–35; emphasis added)

The structure of this pericope is as follows:

[A]   Jesus's family comes to restrain him (3:20–21)
    [B] The scribes come to test Jesus (3:22–30)
[A'] Jesus's family remains outside (3:31–35)

In this sandwich construction, Mark skillfully draws a connection between two claims made by two different groups operating in the spheres of Jesus's public activity. The family of Jesus appears in the two outer frames of the story while the scribes appear in the inner portion. Each makes a claim about Jesus that is out of keeping with what the narrative audience knows to be true.

Often in sandwich stories, Mark draws parallels and contrasts between two characters or character groups, and this unit is no exception. Both groups make parallel claims about Jesus: His family comes to retrieve him because they believe that he is "out of his mind" (3:21), and on a purely social level, one can appreciate this and even regard it as an act of love and concern. Similarly, the scribes insist that Jesus is an emissary of Satan who is able to exorcise demons by Satan's hand (3:22). Again, on a social level, one can understand the chagrin of the scribes, who see Jesus gaining authority at their expense (cf. 1:27–28). However, at the narrative level, both claims are incorrect and, as Jesus suggests, the latter borders on the blasphemous (3:28–30). From the overarching christological perspective of the narrative (1:1; 8:29; 15:39), both groups misidentify Jesus, and they apparently do so because of some supposed flaw in his public behavior. Despite their differences, both groups are depicted in a negative light and are connected by virtue of their errant claims about Jesus.

But the groups also stand in contrast to one another in important ways. First, one group represents his closest familial relations, while the other is a consistent combatant throughout Mark's Gospel. The family of Jesus seeks to "seize" him out of a genuine concern while the scribes accuse and debate with him out of a developing sense of rivalry. Ultimately, both groups display an opposition to Jesus's mission, and therefore to God. True discipleship—and, for Jesus, "true family"—is found in those who do the will of God. The failure of both groups to do so is what creates the occasion for this lesson about following God.

What is perhaps most striking about this text is Jesus's insistence that familial bonds do not guarantee one's closeness to him. On this point, Mark again employs an insider-outsider rhetoric as the suspected insiders (Jesus's family) remain on the outside (spatially, but also relationally) while Jesus is inside describing for his followers the criterion for being a part of his true family. A further implication of this passage is that doing the will of the God may also include the renunciation of one's family. We see even at this early stage that the demands of discipleship are exacting: you become a follower by doing the will of God, which is yet to be fully defined, and potentially by renouncing those who are closest to you for the sake of the gospel.

3. Denying Oneself

Other explicit instructions about discipleship appear in the scene immediately following Jesus's first passion prediction (8:31). After Peter's rebuke of Jesus, and Jesus's counter-rebuke (8:32–33), we read:

> He called the crowd with his disciples, and said to them, "If any want to become my followers, _let them deny themselves and take up their cross and follow me_. For those who want to save their life will lose it, and those who lose their life for my sake, and for the sake of the gospel, will save it. For what will it profit them to gain the whole world and forfeit their life? Indeed, what can they give in return for their life? Those who are ashamed of me and of my words in this adulterous and sinful generation, of them the Son of Man will also be ashamed when he comes in the glory of his Father with the holy angels." (8:34–38; emphasis added)

The directive in 8:34 emphasizes the prior content of Jesus's passion prediction while putting the onus on would-be followers to deny themselves to the point of losing their lives.

The very image of cross-bearing implies difficulty, pain, and suffering. Disciples must be willing to give up everything—their very lives—to follow Jesus. This "call to discipleship is paradoxically both a call to a self-gift unto death and a summons to life" through the suffering and vindicated Jesus.[4] Also connected to self-denial is a steadfast identification with Jesus and his teachings. Here Jesus introduces the negative implications of "shame" for the disciples. They must not be ashamed of the one whom they have followed.[5] This is a summons to boldness amidst suffering and may reflect a scenario in the world behind the text in which those who confessed Christ were being persecuted for their faith.

Just after the second passion prediction in 9:31, we again see explicit instructions about what it means to follow Jesus:

> Then they came to Capernaum; and when he was in the house he asked them, "What were you arguing about on the way?" But they were silent, for on the way they had argued with one another who was the greatest. He sat down, called the twelve, and said to them, "Whoever wants to be first must be last of all and servant of all." Then he took a little child and put it among them; and taking it in his arms, he said to them, "_Whoever welcomes one such child in my name welcomes me, and whoever welcomes me welcomes not me but the one who sent me_." (9:33–37; emphasis added)

In this text, we see that the Twelve have miscalculated because they are thinking of their role in terms of the benefits that

---

4. Francis J. Moloney, *The Gospel of Mark: A Commentary* (Peabody, MA: Hendrickson, 2002), 176.

5. In 13:11, Jesus tells the disciples, "Whenever you are arrested and brought to trial, do not worry beforehand about what to say. Just say whatever is given you at the time, for it is not you speaking, but the Holy Spirit" (NIV). This is another instance of the disciples being advised to move forward boldly despite opposition.

will accrue to them as followers of the Messiah. But discipleship is not about self-aggrandizement. Rather, as we saw in
8:34, following Jesus is ultimately about self-denial. Such an
approach entails putting aside the ambitions of adulthood,
such as rank and prominence, and welcoming those (like
children) without means or social status as you would welcome the Messiah and Son of God. To do so is to welcome
God and participate in his mission.

4. Persevering Until the End (Mark 13:12–13)

In Mark 13, Jesus is positioned opposite the Jewish
temple on the Mount of Olives as he begins to instruct four
of his disciples about things to come. He describes a series of
catastrophic events including the destruction of the temple
complex (13:2), the rise of deceivers claiming to be the Messiah
(13:5–6), wars, rumors of wars, nations rising against nations
(13:7–8), earthquakes, famines (13:8), and civic trials, arrests,
and beatings (13:9–11). All of this is accompanied by extreme
family conflict over devotion to Jesus (13:12). Here Jesus again
provides explicit instructions related to discipleship: "Brother
will betray brother to death, and a father his child, and children will rise against parents and have them put to death; and
you will be hated by all because of my name. *But the one who
endures to the end will be saved*" (13:12–13; emphasis added).

As we reflect on the cumulative theology of discipleship
to this point (as seen in the Gospel's vocabulary), we see
that following Jesus entails (1) leaving one's current world
behind, (2) doing the will of God, (3) boldly adhering to
Jesus's teaching, and (4) displaying a willingness to suffer
even unto death. These are the things to which Jesus now
calls his followers to "endure to the end." Ironically, we will
see that the Twelve—four of whom are addressed directly in
Mark 13—will ultimately fail to endure in these aspects of

discipleship. They will fail to do the will of God. They will abandon Jesus in fear for their own lives. Judas will betray him. Peter will deny knowing him three times. None of them will be present at the foot of the cross, and all will be missing from the scene at the empty tomb. By contrast, a small group of female followers will endure, witness the crucifixion (15:40–41), and receive the good news of Jesus's resurrection from the angelic messenger (16:6–7).

Perseverance implies difficulty. The command to "endure to the end" is intimately connected to Jesus's previous instructions about self-denial, carrying one's cross, family renunciation, and suffering. A true disciple will persevere in the midst of all forms of persecution and threat: family conflict, imprisonment, war, and even natural disasters. Mark envisions a time of forthcoming difficulty during which followers must cling boldly and defiantly to their faith commitments and to the teaching of Jesus. This sort of gritty determination lies at the heart of the Markan understanding of discipleship.

5. "On the Way"

At the midway point of the Gospel, the focus shifts from the day-to-day ministry of Jesus to his impending death. Jesus predicts his rejection and execution three different times (8:31; 9:31; 10:32–34) to prepare his disciples for what will come. We begin to see a more pronounced emphasis on "the way" (Greek: *hodos*; this term is also used for "street" or "road"), which becomes a kind of technical term for Jesus's march toward the cross in Jerusalem throughout the second half of the Gospel. We see an initial hint of this theme in 1:2–3, where the composite scriptural citation introduces John the Baptist as the one sent to prepare "your [i.e., God's] way" (1:2; Greek: *tēn hodon sou*) and "prepare the way of the Lord" (1:3; Greek: *tēn hodon kyriou*). In the Gospel, these phrases are coterminous with the way in which Jesus executes his mission from God. The term is also used in the LXX as a shorthand for obeying God's commands (cf. Exod 32:8; Deut 5:33). Through his ministry and march to the cross, Jesus is going to show us what the "way of the Lord" looks like. This proleptic announcement about the way of God in 1:2–3 prepares the audience for this coming theme across the latter half of the Gospel. The shape of this way becomes clear only as we see Jesus draw ever closer to the cross.

In the second half of the Gospel (8:31–16:8), we see an increasing emphasis on the way and what it means to follow Jesus. The disciples argue "on the way" about who will be the greatest (9:33–34). While "on the way" to Jerusalem, Jesus begins to unveil his future suffering to the disciples in greater detail (10:32–34). After his healing, Bartimaeus ignores Jesus's instructions to depart from him and begins following him "on the way" (10:52). When he finally arrives in Jerusalem for his triumphal entry, Jesus is greeted by the spreading of garments "on the road" in honor of his arrival (11:8). This last example may be intended as a *double entendre* as Jesus is entering on a "road," but his march to Jerusalem has been a march "on the way" to his death.

For our understanding of Mark's theology of discipleship, we cannot overlook the language of following Jesus "on the way" to his crucifixion. This way is both a journey and a programmatic agenda. As we have come to expect to this point in our discussion, following Jesus on the way entails rejection and suffering. But we will ultimately see that it is a redemptive suffering. To follow Jesus on the way is to accept a path characterized by self-denial, bold confidence in identifying with Jesus, upholding his teaching, doing the will of God, and displaying a willingness to endure suffering to the point of giving up your very life.

TO IMITATE THE TWELVE (OR NOT)

In chapter 6, we briefly discussed Mark's negative portrayal of the Twelve. It is important to point out, however, that the characterization of the disciples across the Gospel is more complex than the previous analysis suggests. In addition to the numerous times when the Twelve fail miserably or display theological incomprehension, there are also instances when they show great promise. A balanced treatment of their role will consider both sets of data. That the disciples start out so well but finish so poorly is important for the audience. What does this ambiguous characterization have to tell us about Mark's theology of discipleship? At the very least, it provides an example for the Markan audience of *what not to do*.

In her recent monograph, *The First Biography of Jesus*, Helen Bond has argued that Jesus, rather than his followers, should be regarded as the only true model of discipleship in Mark (see more on this below).[6] In fact, she argues that the idea of the Twelve as models of discipleship would have been completely foreign to the reading experience of Mark's earliest readers. These judgements are based on her conviction that Mark is an ancient Greco-Roman biography (or *bios*), and as such, follows expected genre conventions, one of which is an identification with and imitation of the main character portrayed in the work. In other words, readers who approach Mark according to its classification as a *bios* would necessarily identify with and seek to imitate Jesus, but they are unlikely to have identified with the disciples. She writes, "Authors [of *bioi*] expected a certain level of 'identification' with the protagonist, in that audiences were encouraged to

---

6. Helen Bond, *The First Biography of Jesus: Genre and Meaning in Mark's Gospel* (Grand Rapids: Eerdmans, 2020).

distill the hero's virtues and to apply them to their own lives, but it would be unusual to focus the same level of attention onto the supporting cast."[7] Later in the same discussion she concludes, "All of this means that it was not only inappropriate but also unnecessary for an ancient audience to look to the Twelve as examples of discipleship."[8] I have at least two responses to these claims.

First, I am not fully convinced that Mark fits as neatly into the *bios* genre category as Bond has argued. While it seems clear that Mark has employed *some of the generic elements* of the Greco-Roman biography, and especially its overarching literary framework, he also departs from it in other significant ways. In places, Bond is so enthusiastic in her attempts to establish Mark as a *bios* that some of her interpretations are forced. Though we must admit that there is no "pure example" of the *bios* genre, we must also admit that Mark does not match up in numerous ways with the more commonly cited examples from Plutarch and others. In places, it feels as though Bond wants to force a square peg into a round hole. Second, as careful and compelling as I find much of Bond's treatment of Mark, it is implausible to me that the earliest Christian audiences of this text would have encountered the successes and failures of the Twelve without immediately thinking of the potential implications for their own attempts to follow Jesus. Earliest followers of Jesus would have been aware of how difficult the Markan call to discipleship was, especially in a social setting that was hostile to Christianity. Thus, Mark's disciples emerge as a character group with which real-life disciples certainly could have and likely would have sympathized. Here I am following a long line of scholars

---

7. Bond, *The First Biography of Jesus*, 193.
8. Bond, *The First Biography of Jesus*, 196.

who regard the narrative treatment of the disciples as a key component to Mark's theology of discipleship. To further unveil Mark's ambiguous treatment of the Twelve, we will examine their successes and failures alongside each other.

The Promise of the Twelve (Mark 1–3, 6, 8)

As we trace the progress of the Twelve throughout the story, we should first acknowledge how quickly and unreservedly they follow Jesus after he calls them. In 1:16–17, Jesus calls Peter and Andrew to follow him. Their response is telling: "And immediately they left their nets and followed him" (1:18). This pattern is repeated in the next two verses as Jesus calls James and John, the sons of Zebedee (1:19), who "left their father Zebedee in the boat with the hired men, and followed him" (1:20). Levi displays the same immediacy when Jesus calls him to follow in 2:13–14. These developments represent an auspicious start for the early disciples within the narrative.

In 3:13–19, Jesus goes up onto a mountain and appoints the Twelve by name. There he commissions them (1) to be with him, (2) to preach, and (3) to have authority to cast out demons (3:14–15). Later in 6:7–13, 30—a passage that serves as the bookend to the calling of the Twelve in Mark 3—the disciples are finally sent out to perform the ministerial duties to which they have been appointed. The report they give when they return points to their immediate success: "The apostles gathered around Jesus, and told him all that they had done and taught" (6:30).

At the so-called turning point of the Gospel, Jesus and the Twelve are in Caesarea Philippi, where he asks them: "Who do people say that I am?" They respond, "John the Baptist; and others, Elijah; and still others, one of the prophets." When he asks them who they think he is, Peter responds, "You are the Messiah" (8:27–30). As discussed in previous chapters, this is a critical moment as one of the key minor characters confesses something of theological import about Jesus. The interaction between Jesus and Peter will devolve from here, but for the moment, Peter has correctly assessed and proclaimed Jesus's identity. We cannot overlook this.

Throughout these first few chapters, the disciples appear in a substantially positive light. Mark 4 begins the slow, steady decline of the Twelve, despite a few glimmering moments of hope in Mark 6 and 8. In this way, the Markan disciples appear to mirror the second example from the parable of the sower, as we discussed in chapter 4. Jesus proclaims:

> Other seed fell on rocky ground, where it did not have much soil, and it sprang up quickly, since it had no depth of soil. And when the sun rose, it was scorched; and since it had no root, it withered away. (4:5–6)

In his explanation of the parable, Jesus connects the seed on rocky ground to a group of people who hear the word and respond with an initial enthusiasm but which ultimately result in fruitlessness:

> And these are the ones sown on rocky ground: when they hear the word, they immediately receive it with joy. But they have no root, and endure only for a while; then, when trouble or persecution arises on account of the word, immediately they fall away. (4:16–17)

The Markan disciples are perhaps the perfect narrative fulfillment of this parabolic description. They begin with the great promise of enthusiastic abandon. They leave their lives and professions to follow Jesus with immediacy and passion. But as he begins to unveil the details of his identity and the demands of his call to follow, they reveal their lack of depth and ultimately fall away when faced with the trouble and persecution that following Jesus requires. The Twelve receive the message of Jesus with joy but ultimately fail to endure.

The Failures of the Twelve (Mark 4, 8–16)

The failures of the Markan disciples are well documented:

1. The Twelve display an inability to understand Jesus's parables. He seems surprised by this and asks: "Do you not understand this parable? Then how will you understand all the parables?" (4:13). This is an initial indication of their theological incomprehension, though it is only made clearer by following their narrative development going forward.

2. Jesus and the Twelve are on a boat when a huge storm arises. They cry out to him but seemingly without an awareness of his capabilities. Jesus awakens, calms the storm, and then questions the disciples: He said to them, "Why are you afraid? Have you still no faith?" And they were filled with great awe and said to one another, "Who then is this, that even the wind and the sea obey him?" (4:40–41).

3. In 6:30–44, Jesus feeds the multitude of five thousand with five barley loaves and two fish. Again in 8:1–10, Jesus and the Twelve are faced with a hungry multitude— this time four thousand—and the disciples ask, "How can one feed these people with bread here in the desert?" (8:4). This would not be a silly question if this were the first time such a scenario had arisen. But Jesus has already fed a much bigger crowd in a similar setting. The audience knows this and is left to wonder why the

Twelve do not immediately return to that moment to provide an answer to their own question.

4. After Peter's declaration that Jesus is the Messiah (8:29), Jesus begins instructing the Twelve about the fate he must suffer at the hands of the religious leaders. The rejection and suffering he will undergo is at the heart of his messianic mission. When Peter objects to this mission, Jesus responds, "Get behind me, Satan! For you are setting your mind not on divine things but on human things" (8:33). Peter's big moment has been tainted by his focus on the things of this world. His acknowledgement that Jesus is the Messiah (8:29) is a moment of promise, but it is followed by a moment of extreme disappointment and failure.

5. In 9:14–29, Jesus heals a young boy with an unclean spirit. This event is set in the context of a dispute between the Twelve and the scribes. When Jesus inquires about the argument that has taken place, a man in the crowd responds: "Teacher, I brought you my son; he has a spirit that makes him unable to speak; and whenever it seizes him, it dashes him down; and he foams and grinds his teeth and becomes rigid; and I asked your disciples to cast it out, but they could not do so" (9:17–18). We recall that when the Twelve were sent out in 6:7–13, 30, part of their mission was to cast out unclean spirits. They experienced initial success in these endeavors, but now they are unable to do so. This narrative cue alerts us to the continuing devolution of the Twelve.

6. After Jesus's second passion prediction in 9:31, we read that the disciples were arguing on the way to Capernaum about who among them would be the greatest. How can they be focused on their own individual

greatness in the face of two predictions about Jesus's rejection and execution?

7. In the latter chapters of the Gospel, we also begin to see the foibles of individual members of the Twelve. In 10:35–45, the sons of Zebedee, James and John, request to sit at the right and left side of Jesus when he comes into his glory. Their request represents a fundamental misunderstanding of Jesus's mission. It is not about glory. It is about suffering. At this request, the other disciples are understandably indignant. In 14:10–11, Judas Iscariot agrees to betray Jesus. In 14:27–31, Jesus predicts that all will abandon him, but Peter proclaims that he is prepared to abide with Jesus, even unto death. Jesus responds with a prediction that Peter will deny him three times before morning.

8. During Jesus's arrest in the garden (14:43–52), Judas the betrayer arrives with a group of men to take Jesus into custody. Chaos ensues and Mark provides this succinct piece of narration: "All of them deserted him and fled" (14:50).

9. In 14:66–72, Jesus's earlier prediction of Peter's threefold denial comes to pass. The denial itself is a problem, but details of the entire interaction are devastating for Peter's portrayal. He is outside warming himself by the fire while Jesus is inside being condemned (14:67). A servant girl accuses Peter of being one of the associates of Jesus. He responds, "I do not know or understand what you are talking about" (14:68). The rooster crows for the first time after this denial. The servant girl accuses him again in 14:69, and again he denies it. This culminates in other bystanders accusing Peter of being a Galilean. Mark narrates Peter's final response in the following way:

> But he began to curse, and he swore an oath, "I do
> not know this man you are talking about." At that
> moment the cock crowed for the second time. Then
> Peter remembered that Jesus had said to him, "Be-
> fore the cock crows twice, you will deny me three
> times." And he broke down and wept. (14:71–72)

After this point, we no longer see any of the Twelve disciples
in the narrative. They have all abandoned Jesus. None of
them will be there at the moment of his crucifixion. None of
them will be there to witness his resurrection. However, perhaps there is still a hint of promise for the Twelve indicated
in the proclamation of the angelic messenger at the empty
tomb: "But *go, tell his disciples and Peter* that he is going ahead
of you to Galilee; there you will see him, just as he told you"
(16:7; emphasis added). Though the Twelve have abandoned
him, there is still hope for their rehabilitation.

One of the best ways to learn how to do something is to
watch someone do it well. Another effective way to learn how
to do something well is to watch someone do it poorly. In some
ways, the Twelve are the perfect example of how *not to follow
Jesus*, but despite their failures, the narrative ends on a note
of potential hope for them. This is a message for an audience
of would-be disciples that even in the face of grave missteps,
hope abounds for those committed to following Jesus.

TO IMITATE JESUS (OR NOT)

Above I took issue with the some of the claims in Helen
Bond's recent book, *The First Biography of Jesus*. In places she
overstates her case for understanding Mark as an example of
Greco-Roman biography. However, it seems clear that Mark
has, at the very least, employed the storytelling framework

of the *bios* genre, even while incorporating other generic elements of ancient literature. Therefore, I believe Bond makes an important contribution in emphasizing that earliest readers would likely have *identified with Jesus* as an imitable example. This insight has been overlooked and even dismissed outright in previous discussions of discipleship in Mark. Scholars routinely reject the idea of imitating Jesus by asking things like, "Does Mark want his audience to try walking on water?" or "Will Mark's readers attempt to heal the sick or raise the dead?" Bond deftly responds to such objections by noting that:

> The imitation of the heroes of biographies does not mean following every detail of their lives, but rather seeing their character and moulding one's life on that. Thus Mark's readers are no more called upon to walk on water than readers of Plutarch's generals to engage in battle, or readers of Philostratus' *Life of Apollonius of Tyana* are to acquire miraculous powers. It is taken for granted that the hero is far superior to any who might come after him; what is important is that readers take away the character and way of life of the hero, and model themselves on that.[9]

To my mind, this claim is compelling and largely correct. So we must ask, What elements of Jesus's life and vocation would earliest readers have sought to emulate? We can identify at least three here.

1. Compassion for the Sick and Suffering

One of the most distinctive elements of the Markan Jesus's ministry is his care for the marginalized. On numerous

---

9. Bond, *The First Biography of Jesus*, 196–97.

occasions he heals the sick and suffering (1:29–32, 40–45; 2:1–12; 3:1–6; 5:21–43; 6:53–56; 7:24–30, 31–37; 8:22–26; 9:14–29; 10:46–52) or provides for those in need (6:37–44; 8:1–10). Importantly, Jesus is occasionally said to perform these actions with compassion. We have abundant evidence of ancient healers in both Jewish and Greco-Roman circles. These include well-known figures associated with the cult of Asclepius and Jewish figures such as Honi the Circle Drawer, Eleazar, and Hanina ben Dosa, just to name a few. In general, language connected to emotions is very sparse in the accounts of these healers, and significantly, none of them portray their healer as displaying pity or compassion. On this count, the Markan Jesus appears to be unique.[10] Consider the following examples in which the Greek verbs *splanchnizomai* (to have compassion/pity) or *eleeō* (to have mercy) are employed:

1. Just before the first feeding miracle in 6:37–44, Jesus and the disciples encounter the multitude of five thousand and Mark notes: "As he went ashore, he saw a great crowd; *and he had compassion* [Greek: *esplanchnisthē*] *for them*, because they were like sheep without a shepherd; and he began to teach them many things" (6:34; emphasis added). This emotional response on the part of Jesus leads directly to the multiplication of fish and loaves.

2. When Jesus encounters the second multitude in Mark

---

10. Mark presents Jesus with a full range of emotions, including anger (1:41; 3:5), grief (3:5), amazement (6:6), compassion/pity (6:34; 8:2), indignation (10:14), love (10:21), deep distress (14:33), agitation (14:33), and overwhelming sorrow (14:34). Mark also pictures Jesus issuing stern warnings (1:34) and sighing deeply (7:34; 8:12). I am indebted to my former student, Dr. Jonathan Bryant, whose insightful work on the characterization of Mark's Jesus as a compassionate healer has significantly informed my own thinking about this subject. See the published version of his dissertation, *Compassion and the Characterization of the Markan Jesus*, BibInt 223 (Leiden: Brill, 2024).

8, we read: "In those days when there was again a great crowd without anything to eat, he called his disciples and said to them, "*I have compassion* [Greek: *splanchnizomai*] *for the crowd*, because they have been with me now for three days and have nothing to eat. If I send them away hungry to their homes, they will faint on the way—and some of them have come from a great distance" (8:1–3; emphasis added). Again, Jesus's emotional response leads to the multiplication of food for the entire multitude.

3. In Mark 9, a father brings his ailing son to Jesus. The boy is possessed by a spirit that causes him to have seizures, fall to the ground, and grind his teeth. Upon seeing Jesus, the boy falls down and begins to foam at the mouth. A conversation between Jesus and the boy's father ensues:

> Jesus asked the father, "How long has this been happening to him?" And he said, "From childhood. It has often cast him into the fire and into the water, to destroy him; but if you are able to do anything, *have pity* [Greek: *splanchnistheis*] on us and help us." Jesus said to him, "If you are able!—All things can be done for the one who believes." Immediately the father of the child cried out, "I believe; help my unbelief!" (9:21–24; emphasis added)

In response to this request, Jesus heals the young boy. Given what we have seen elsewhere in the Gospel, it is not a coincidence that Mark narrates this healing in the context of a request for compassion.

4. In Mark 10, Jesus encounters a blind beggar named Bartimaeus who shouts out, "Son of David, have mercy

[Greek: *eleēson*] on me!" (10:48). In response to this plea, Jesus learns that Bartimaeus wants to receive his sight and Jesus says to him: "Go; your faith has made you well." Immediately he regained his sight and followed him on the way (10:52). Here we have another instance of Jesus acting out of a plea for compassion.

The Markan Jesus models, in part, what a virtuous life looks like by continually crossing cultural boundaries in response to human need. He responds to this need in a miraculous manner but also in a way that is worthy of being emulated by Mark's audience. Followers of Jesus may not be able to perform healings or other miraculous deeds, but they are certainly capable of displaying compassion and pity toward those in need.

2. A Life of Self-Denial

The command to "take up one's cross" (8:34), while foreshadowing Jesus's redemptive death at the end of the Gospel, is also a metaphor for the type of behavior that Jesus models throughout his ministry. This includes (1) the willingness to renounce the things in life that distract from following God, including family, and (2) an endurance in the face of opposition. Above we examined the text in which Jesus establishes a "new family" (3:20–35), and in the process renounces the family that has misjudged his behavior while coming to "seize him." Followers of Jesus must be prepared to endure loss of family and social status, as well as rejection by those with power and influence.

This life of self-denial also includes a willingness to forgo one's prerogatives for the greater good. Throughout Mark, Jesus is continually proclaimed as the Son of God. But what we see is his constant willingness to set aside any claims to glory or privilege so that he may "give his life a ransom for many" (10:45). This setting aside of divine prerogatives is taken a step further in that the Son of God is also willing to suffer for the sake of the Gospel and the kingdom. The virtuous, imitable life that Jesus lives reverses our expectations and reveals a concern for the greater good above the needs of the individual—even if that individual is the very Son of God!

3. Courage in the Face of Death

In this chapter, we have already established that a key component of the call to discipleship in Mark is the willingness to suffer to the point of giving up one's life. Throughout this book, we have also argued that suffering is at the heart of Jesus's messianic mission (cf. 8:31; 9:31; 10:32–45). While the Twelve will fail to endure to the end (14:50; cf. 13:12–13), Jesus will ultimately face his death courageously and thereby fulfill his God-ordained mission (cf. 14:36). In this way, Jesus does exactly what he calls his followers to do. He models a noble death at the hands of his enemies, those opposing the will of God.

FOLLOWING THROUGH A MARKAN LENS

While Mark's Gospel shares some features with other ancient approaches to discipleship, it also has its own distinctive shape. To follow Jesus is to be "on the way" to a cross-shaped life characterized by sacrificial self-giving. True disciples will give up their claims to earthly status and money. We see this illustrated not only in the call of the earliest disciples but also in Jesus's own willingness to forgo divine prerogatives. True disciples will also cling to the teachings of Jesus and endure until the end, even if the end requires suffering or death. We see this illustrated poorly in the failure of the Twelve to endure. But we also see it illustrated well by the women at the empty tomb and by Jesus in his march toward the cross. The path to following the Markan Jesus is one beset by suffering and vindication. Those who endure will be rewarded and, as we saw in the angelic proclamation in 16:6–7, there is hope even for those who have fallen away in the face of such demands.

FOR FURTHER READING

A. Narrative Critical Readings of the Disciples, Narrative Characterization as Discipleship

Carey, Holly J. "Women in Action: Models for Discipleship in Mark's Gospel." *CBQ* 81.4 (2019): 430–48.

Malbon, Elizabeth Struthers. "Disciples/Crowds/Whoever: Markan Characters and Readers." *NovT* 28.2 (1986): 104–30.

Malbon, Elizabeth Struthers. "Fallible Followers: Men and Women in the Gospel of Mark." *Sem* 28 (1983): 29–48.

Tannehill, Robert C. "The Disciples in Mark: The Function of a Narrative Role." *JR* 57.4 (1977): 386–405.

Williams, Joel F. *Other Followers of Jesus: Minor Characters as Major Figures in Mark's Gospel.* JSNTSup 102. Sheffield: JSOT Press, 1994.

B. Redaction Critical Readings of the Disciples

Best, Ernest. *Disciples and Discipleship: Studies in the Gospel According to Mark.* London: T&T Clark, 1986.

Best, Ernest. *Following Jesus: Discipleship in the Gospel of Mark.* JSNTSup 4. Sheffield: JSOT Press, 1981.

Black, C. Clifton. *The Disciples According to Mark: Markan Redaction in Current Debate.* 2nd ed. Grand Rapids: Eerdmans, 2012.

Tyson, Joseph B. "The Blindness of the Disciples in Mark." *JBL* 80.3 (1961): 261–68.

C. Theological Readings of the Disciples, Discipleship

Green, Joel B. *The Way of the Cross: Following Jesus in the Gospel of Mark.* Nashville: Abingdon, 1991.

Hays, Richard B. "The Way of the Cross: Following Jesus in the
    Gospel of Mark." In *Cruciform Scripture: Cross, Participation,
    Mission*, edited by Christopher W. Skinner, Nijay K. Gupta,
    Andy Johnson, and Drew Strait, 22–36. Grand Rapids:
    Eerdmans, 2020.
Henderson, Suzanne Watts. *Christology and Discipleship in the Gospel
    of Mark*. SNTSMS 135. Cambridge, UK: Cambridge University
    Press, 2006.
Hurtado, Larry W. "Following Jesus in the Gospel of Mark—and
    Beyond." In *Patterns of Discipleship in the New Testament*, edited
    by Richard N. Longenecker, 9–28. McMaster New Testament
    Studies. Grand Rapids: Eerdmans, 1996.

Acknowledgments

A multitude of colleagues and friends have contributed to this book. First, I want to express my thanks to Nijay Gupta and Katya Covrett for their invitation to contribute this volume to the New Word Biblical Themes Series. I am grateful for their helpful editorial suggestions along the way. I would also like to thank Zach Eberhart, Shane Gormley, Meghan Henning, Raleigh Heth, Anthony Le Donne, Daniel McClellan, Francis J. Moloney, Elizabeth Shively, Olivia Stewart Lester, and Sam Won, all of whom either discussed my research with me or read portions of the manuscript and offered helpful feedback. Kelly Iverson and Paul Wheatley both read the entire manuscript and offered insights that improved the book. As always, any mistakes or deficiencies that remain in this book are solely my responsibility.

My friend Rafael Rodriguez proved to be a faithful conversation partner as I worked out a number of ideas in this book. I am grateful to Rafael for his friendship and for the opportunity to have our almost weekly conversations about teaching and scholarship regularly veer into the more important and complex issues associated with raising our children. Another friend and colleague, Josh Jipp, consistently enriches my life in the Chicagoland area with his stellar conversation, excellent taste in music, terrible sports opinions, and generally robust friendship. I am also privileged to count two exceptional gospels scholars among my personal friends and colleagues—Mark Goodacre and James Barker. Conversations with them in recent years, along with opportunities to read their works in progress, have significantly informed my understanding of the canonical gospels.

I am especially appreciative of my departmental colleagues in our biblical studies section in the theology department at Loyola University Chicago—Bob DiVito, Brian Lee, Edmondo Lupieri, Olivia Stewart Lester, and Tom Wetzel. Working alongside them each day gives my vocational life a unique shape and character of which I would otherwise be sorely deprived.

One of the joys of my job is that I get to spend time working with gifted graduate students, many of whom are Jesuit scholastics. During the spring semester of 2022, I ran an independent study with Hunter D'Armond, SJ, where we spent an hour each week working through the Greek text of Mark's Gospel and reveling in the text-critical, grammatical, and syntactical challenges it presents. Our close attention to the nuances of the text that semester helped prepare me mentally to enter the process of writing this book. Sincere thanks are also due to my former MA student, Sarah Buntin, who served as my research assistant during the 2018–2019 academic year. Sarah dutifully culled decades of published books and articles to assist me with my research for this book and another project on Mark's Christology. I am grateful for her diligent and comprehensive work.

I also want to acknowledge the careful engagement of two of my chapters offered by the members of the New Testament and Early Christianity Colloquium in the theology department at Loyola in the spring of 2023.

As ever, I am most indebted to my wife, Tara, the love

of my life and my true companion for these past twenty-seven years. She is the source of the greatest joys in my life, and those include our three children Christopher, Abigail, and Andrew, without whom I would not know what it means to love. Together, the four of them give my life profound meaning and purpose.

Subject Index

Scripture Index/Index of Ancient Sources